# Nelson Caribbean

# Multiple Choice Tests for Common Entrance

# English

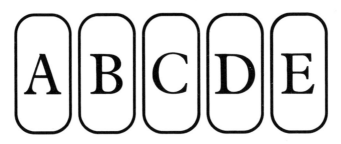

P Wint · F Sangster · D Blackwood

G000069246

Nelson Thornes

Text © Freda Sangster, Phyllis Wint and Delores Blackwood, 1983

The right of Freda Sangster, Phyllis Wint and Delores Blackwood to be identified as author of this work has been asserted by them in accordance with the Copyright, Designs and Patents Act 1988.

All rights reserved. No part of this publication may be reproduced or transmitted in any form or by any means, electronic or mechanical, including photocopy, record-ing or any information storage and retrieval system, without permission in writing from the publisher or under licence from the Copyright Licensing Agency Limited, of Saffron House, 6-10 Kirby Street, London, EC1N 8TS

Any person who commits any unauthorised act in relation to this publication may be liable to criminal prosecution and civil claims for damages.

First published in 1983 by:
Nelson Thornes Ltd
Delta Place
27 Bath Road
CHELTENHAM
GL53 7TH
United Kingdom

13 / 25 24

A catalogue record for this book is available from the British Library

ISBN 978 0 17 566322 4

Printed by Multivista Global Ltd

# CONTENTS

## ACKNOWLEDGEMENTS

We would like to acknowledge the kind assistance of the following people who have helped to make this book a reality:

Mrs Doreen Bell for her encouragement and who patiently typed and retyped the manuscript.
Husbands George and William for their confidence and encouragement.
Mrs S. Robinson for her passage on Carnival.
All our colleagues who encouraged us.

# INSTRUCTIONS
# TO TEACHERS AND STUDENTS

This book contains eight papers of 100 questions each. As you can see, every page has five columns of ovals bearing the letters A, B, C, D and E. You should answer each question by shading in the oval which contains the letter corresponding to the capital letter in bold type beside the answer you think is the correct one.

In the examination, your paper will be marked by computer. To give you practice in answering a computerised examination paper, this book is laid out in the same way as the Common Entrance examination paper will be.

A computer is a machine and cannot make judgements in the way a human examiner can—it will not be able to understand small inconsistencies. So it is very important that you understand how to complete the tests correctly.

Take a soft pencil and shade in the oval which you think has the correct answer. Be sure to shade in all of the oval, so that it is completely covered. If you don't the computer may fail to record your mark! Be careful not to make any stray mark on the paper or the computer may misread it.

If you feel that you have made a mistake and want to correct it, remember to use a rubber to erase the pencil mark before you shade in the correct oval.

Here is an example:

Just as we turned the corner the car fell into an enormous crater. Our chauffeur clambered from the car quickly to investigate what sounded like permanent damage. His assumption was accurate. The front of the car was beyond repair. All efforts to remove it proved futile. Dusk was fast approaching, so one could appreciate the anxiety of its occupants.

**1** When did the accident take place?
**A** just as we turned the corner
**B** in an enormous crater
**C** at dusk
**D** at noon
**E** that day

We shade in (A) because the accident took place 'just as we turned the corner'. Now try this:

Choose the word which could be substituted for the underlined word in the sentence.

**2 They were dismissed from the dining room because of their rough behaviour.**
**A** quick   **B** crude   **C** wicked   **D** teasing   **E** untidy

(A)   (B)   (C)   (D)   (E)

We shade in (B) because 'crude' means the same as 'rough'.

Each paper should take you one hour. You know that there are 100 questions in every paper, so remember to use your time carefully. Don't spend too long on any one question. If you cannot answer a question, leave it and try again at the end.

Teachers should note that the answers are on the four-page spread between pages 40 and 41. They may be detached and kept separate from the book if they so wish.

Good Luck!

# PAPER ONE

Read the following passage carefully, then answer the questions in the answer column.

Slowly the sun sinks in the west and the light of day will soon be fading. The gold and crimson heralds the ending day and the sky seems to blaze with colours. Then suddenly, the glory fades, the shadows lengthen and the night approaches. Another day has ended majestically.

1 **The time of day is**
   **A** dawn **B** noon **C** sunset **D** night
   **E** early morning

   Ⓐ Ⓑ Ⓒ Ⓓ Ⓔ

2 **The sky appears**
   **A** brightly coloured **B** dark **C** suddenly **D** grey
   **E** in the west

   Ⓐ Ⓑ Ⓒ Ⓓ Ⓔ

3 **'Heralds' means the same as**
   **A** angels **B** sings **C** colours **D** announces **E** ends

   Ⓐ Ⓑ Ⓒ Ⓓ Ⓔ

4 **You can tell that the writer**
   **A** hates this time of day **B** is annoyed
   **C** does not really care **D** is unconcerned
   **E** loves the sunset

   Ⓐ Ⓑ Ⓒ Ⓓ Ⓔ

5 **'Majestically' means the same as**
   **A** grandly **B** pretty **C** quickly **D** in darkness
   **E** with shadows

   Ⓐ Ⓑ Ⓒ Ⓓ Ⓔ

6 **The 'glory fades' refers to**
   **A** the loss of bright colours **B** getting lighter
   **C** sadness **D** the night **E** the daylight

   Ⓐ Ⓑ Ⓒ Ⓓ Ⓔ

In each of the following sentences choose the word which means the same or nearly the same as the word in capitals.

7 **The rich man CONTRIBUTED a large sum of money to the building fund.**
   **A** begged **B** loaned **C** borrowed **D** gave **E** stole

   Ⓐ Ⓑ Ⓒ Ⓓ Ⓔ

8 **The winning design was CREATED by two young boys.**
   **A** made **B** bought **C** liked **D** brought **E** stolen

   Ⓐ Ⓑ Ⓒ Ⓓ Ⓔ

1

**9** The DELUGE blocked roadways and destroyed much of the farmers' cultivation.
**A** danger  **B** delivery van  **C** heavy rains
**D** high wind  **E** thunder

Ⓐ Ⓑ Ⓒ Ⓓ Ⓔ

**10** John was REQUESTED to be the guest speaker at the function.
**A** chief  **B** asked  **C** told  **D** urged  **E** implored

Ⓐ Ⓑ Ⓒ Ⓓ Ⓔ

**11** The day was cold and HUMID and so we all had to dress carefully for the picnic.
**A** beautiful  **B** dry  **C** wet  **D** gloomy  **E** sunny

Ⓐ Ⓑ Ⓒ Ⓓ Ⓔ

**12** The concert will COMMENCE as soon as the audience is seated.
**A** come  **B** end  **C** finish  **D** begin  **E** fail

Ⓐ Ⓑ Ⓒ Ⓓ Ⓔ

**13** The speaker's voice was AUDIBLE from the back of the room.
**A** loud  **B** not heard  **C** angry  **D** could be heard
**E** gruff

Ⓐ Ⓑ Ⓒ Ⓓ Ⓔ

**14** Mary is the PRINCIPAL character in the school's new play.
**A** pretty  **B** chief  **C** large  **D** headmistress  **E** least

Ⓐ Ⓑ Ⓒ Ⓓ Ⓔ

**15** As the boys travelled along happily, an IMMENSE rock suddenly rolled down the slope, blocking the road.
**A** huge  **B** little  **C** rough  **D** hard  **E** dirty

Ⓐ Ⓑ Ⓒ Ⓓ Ⓔ

**16** We were TERRIFIED when, rounding the corner, we saw the bull coming towards us.
**A** laughing  **B** pleased  **C** angry  **D** frightened
**E** sorry

Ⓐ Ⓑ Ⓒ Ⓓ Ⓔ

**17** The villagers were very HOSTILE to the man they thought had been stealing their cattle.
**A** unfriendly  **B** careful  **C** hospitable  **D** kind
**E** thoughtless

Ⓐ Ⓑ Ⓒ Ⓓ Ⓔ

**18** The hungry man was GRATEFUL for the food given him by the kind woman.
**A** glad  **B** thankful  **C** greedy  **D** displeased
**E** happy

Ⓐ Ⓑ Ⓒ Ⓓ Ⓔ

In each of the following sentences choose the correct spelling for the underlined word.

19  The responsibilities of the goverment of a country are many.
    A. gooverment   B gouverment   C government
    D govirment   E govurnment

⒜ ⒝ ⒞ ⒟ ⒠

20  The ship was blown off its coarse during the storm.
    A corse   B chorse   C course   D coerse   E corese

⒜ ⒝ ⒞ ⒟ ⒠

21  We were all releived when he regained consciousness.
    A releaved   B relieved   C releeved   D reileved
    E releved

⒜ ⒝ ⒞ ⒟ ⒠

22  The girl has a very small waste.
    A waist   B waaste   C wayste   D waiste   E waeste

⒜ ⒝ ⒞ ⒟ ⒠

23  Please use good grammer when you write.
    A gramma   B grammar   C gramar   D graamer
    E gramer

⒜ ⒝ ⒞ ⒟ ⒠

24  Mother rinced the clothes in clean water.
    A rinsed   B rynsed   C rinst   D rensed   E rynced

⒜ ⒝ ⒞ ⒟ ⒠

25  I would be happy if you would seperate the colours for me.
    A seperaate   B sepurate   C sepirate   D separate
    E sepahrate

⒜ ⒝ ⒞ ⒟ ⒠

26  People need to learn that vilence does not solve their problems.
    A violence   B violense   C vilents   D voilence
    E vyolence

⒜ ⒝ ⒞ ⒟ ⒠

27  I cannot except your gift, it is too valuable.
    A expect   B accept   C axept   D axcept   E actsept

⒜ ⒝ ⒞ ⒟ ⒠

Complete the following sentences using the correct word forms of the word in capitals.

28  ALLOW   I am not …… to go out alone at nights.
    A allows   B allowed   C allowance   D allowing
    E allowances

⒜ ⒝ ⒞ ⒟ ⒠

3

29  **FAITH   John has been a ...... worker for many years.**
    **A** faithful   **B** faithless   **C** faithed   **D** fathing
    **E** faiths

Ⓐ  Ⓑ  Ⓒ  Ⓓ  Ⓔ

30  **ATTEND   Mary's ...... at school is perfect. She is
    never absent.**
    **A** attending   **B** attends   **C** attendance   **D** attention
    **E** attendful

Ⓐ  Ⓑ  Ⓒ  Ⓓ  Ⓔ

31  **SEE   My teacher ...... and hears everything that
    happens in the room.**
    **A** sight   **B** seen   **C** saw   **D** sees   **E** seeing

Ⓐ  Ⓑ  Ⓒ  Ⓓ  Ⓔ

32  **ACT   His ...... in the matter was commendable.**
    **A** action   **B** acts   **C** acted   **D** acting   **E** activate

Ⓐ  Ⓑ  Ⓒ  Ⓓ  Ⓔ

33  **CUSTOM   It is ...... to drink sorrel at Christmas time
    in Jamaica.**
    **A** customer   **B** customs   **C** customary
    **D** accustom   **E** accustomed

Ⓐ  Ⓑ  Ⓒ  Ⓓ  Ⓔ

34  **CLEAN   She ...... the furniture every day.**
    **A** cleans   **B** cleaner   **C** cleaning   **D** cleanly   **E** clean

Ⓐ  Ⓑ  Ⓒ  Ⓓ  Ⓔ

35  **CONFIDE   We have ...... in your ability to pass the
    examination.**
    **A** confides   **B** confiding   **C** confidence
    **D** confidences   **E** confided

Ⓐ  Ⓑ  Ⓒ  Ⓓ  Ⓔ

36  **BRAVE   The boy was awarded a medal for his ...... .**
    **A** braves   **B** bravery   **C** braving   **D** braveful
    **E** braved

Ⓐ  Ⓑ  Ⓒ  Ⓓ  Ⓔ

37  **CONFUSE   I am so ...... I do not know what to do.**
    **A** confuses   **B** confusing   **C** confused
    **D** confusion   **E** confuser

Ⓐ  Ⓑ  Ⓒ  Ⓓ  Ⓔ

38  **RECEIVE   The man gave me a ...... when I paid the
    bill.**
    **A** receipt   **B** received   **C** receives   **D** receiver
    **E** receiving

Ⓐ  Ⓑ  Ⓒ  Ⓓ  Ⓔ

39  **GROW   Wild orchids ...... in the woods where we
    camped.**
    **A** grown   **B** grew   **C** growth   **D** grows   **E** growing

Ⓐ  Ⓑ  Ⓒ  Ⓓ  Ⓔ

In each of the following sentences one word is used wrongly. Choose the letter with the correct answer.

40　Between you and I there is no such thing as Santa Claus.
　　A us　B they　C me　D she　E her

Ⓐ Ⓑ Ⓒ Ⓓ Ⓔ

41　Neither Mary or her brother is here today.
　　A nor　B and　C also　D but　E too

Ⓐ Ⓑ Ⓒ Ⓓ Ⓔ

42　Every boy should take their own lunch to school.
　　A our　B mine　C his　D they　E them

Ⓐ Ⓑ Ⓒ Ⓓ Ⓔ

43　John is the biggest of the twins.
　　A big　B bigger　C same size　D identical
　　E smallest

Ⓐ Ⓑ Ⓒ Ⓓ Ⓔ

44　My little sister is almost as tall as me.
　　A us　B I　C we　D they　E them

Ⓐ Ⓑ Ⓒ Ⓓ Ⓔ

45　Everybody were happy when our team won the match.
　　A is　B was　C quite　D are　E has been

Ⓐ Ⓑ Ⓒ Ⓓ Ⓔ

46　It is hour turn to prepare supper tonight.
　　A us　B we　C my　D our　E they

Ⓐ Ⓑ Ⓒ Ⓓ Ⓔ

47　James nose nothing about Algebra.
　　A knows　B new　C know　D learn　E do

Ⓐ Ⓑ Ⓒ Ⓓ Ⓔ

Read the following passage carefully then answer the questions.

The extensive cultivation of sugar-cane in Jamaica is seen in the lush green fields all over the island. Sugar-cane is a versatile crop. From it come rum, molasses, sugar and bagasse board as some of its by-products. Although we see numerous sugar factories around the island, sugar is often scarce and high priced to the Jamaican consumer. The question many are now asking is . . . should we continue growing sugar-cane or could these lands be better utilised?

48　Sugar-cane is grown
　　A only in a few places　B only in St Catherine
　　C only in Westmoreland　D all over the island
　　E nowhere in Jamaica

Ⓐ Ⓑ Ⓒ Ⓓ Ⓔ

5

**49**  **Sugar is**
  **A** always available  **B** often hard to obtain
  **C** is never available  **D** all sold abroad
  **E** only had in Jamaica

**50**  **'Extensive' means**
  **A** always  **B** everywhere  **C** difficult  **D** wide
  **E** fields

**51**  **Sugar factories should be producing**
  **A** more sugar  **B** no sugar  **C** insufficient sugar
  **D** more rum  **E** more molasses

**52**  **A consumer is one who**
  **A** sells goods  **B** window shops  **C** uses the goods
  **D** packs the goods in the warehouse  **E** is a wholesaler

**53**  **'Utilised' means**
  **A** sold  **B** kept  **C** cleared  **D** mulched  **E** used

**54**  **Many people appear to think that we should**
  **A** grow more sugar-cane
  **B** replace sugar with other crops
  **C** buy more sugar  **D** not worry about it
  **E** export more sugar

In each of the following sentences choose the correctly punctuated sentence.

**55**  **A** 'Where are you going,' asked his mother.
  **B** Where, are you going? asked his mother.
  **C** 'Where are you going asked his mother'
  **D** 'Where are you going?' asked his mother.
  **E** 'Where are you going'? asked his mother.

**56**  **A** We had cake, ice cream, fruit punch, popcorn and
    sweets at the party.
  **B** We had cake, ice cream fruit, punch popcorn, and
    sweets at the party.
  **C** We had cake, ice cream, fruit punch, popcorn, and
    sweets at the party.
  **D** We had cake ice cream, fruit punch popcorn, and
    sweets at the party.
  **E** We had cake ice cream fruit punch popcorn and sweets
    at the party.

6

**57**
  **A** Mr Brown, the baker makes delicious cakes.
  **B** Mr Brown, the baker, makes delicious cakes.
  **C** Mr Brown, the baker, makes delicious, cakes.
  **D** Mr Brown the baker, makes delicious cakes.
  **E** Mr Brown the baker makes delicious cakes.

Ⓐ Ⓑ Ⓒ Ⓓ Ⓔ

**58**
  **A** 'Look out, shouted Bob, he is coming'.
  **B** 'Look out!' shouted Bob, 'he is coming.'
  **C** 'Look out, shouted Bob, 'he is coming'
  **D** Look out, shouted Bob, he is coming.
  **E** 'Look out', shouted Bob, 'he is coming!'

Ⓐ Ⓑ Ⓒ Ⓓ Ⓔ

**59**
  **A** The army, marched to the town, the residents had fled.
  **B** The army marched to the town the residents had fled.
  **C** The army marched to the town, the residents had fled.
  **D** The army marched to the town. The residents had fled.
  **E** The army marched, to the town, the residents had fled.

Ⓐ Ⓑ Ⓒ Ⓓ Ⓔ

Choose the word that is nearest in meaning to the one in capitals.

**60 TERMINATE**
  **A** begin  **B** end  **C** change  **D** make  **E** determine

Ⓐ Ⓑ Ⓒ Ⓓ Ⓔ

**61 AID**
  **A** promise  **B** hide  **C** change  **D** help  **E** try

Ⓐ Ⓑ Ⓒ Ⓓ Ⓔ

**62 CUSTOM**
  **A** habit  **B** choice  **C** buying  **D** people  **E** few

Ⓐ Ⓑ Ⓒ Ⓓ Ⓔ

**63 APPLAUD**
  **A** stop  **B** clap  **C** talk  **D** proud  **E** rebuke

Ⓐ Ⓑ Ⓒ Ⓓ Ⓔ

**64 ODOUR**
  **A** adore  **B** hold  **C** smell  **D** love  **E** open

Ⓐ Ⓑ Ⓒ Ⓓ Ⓔ

**65 PECULIAR**
  **A** strange  **B** usual  **C** ordinary  **D** happy  **E** fun

Ⓐ Ⓑ Ⓒ Ⓓ Ⓔ

**66 BRILLIANT**
  **A** big  **B** lighted  **C** tall  **D** bright  **E** pleasant

Ⓐ Ⓑ Ⓒ Ⓓ Ⓔ

**67 EXHAUSTED**
  **A** funny  **B** large  **C** weary  **D** tossed  **E** running

Ⓐ Ⓑ Ⓒ Ⓓ Ⓔ

**68  EXPOSE**
    **A** fight  **B** show  **C** quarrel  **D** light  **E** boast

A   B   C   D   E

**69  REMEDY**
    **A** recall  **B** rely  **C** ready  **D** help  **E** cure

A   B   C   D   E

In each of the following choose the correct word to complete the phrase.

**70  ran ...... the road as the car approached**
    **A** in  **B** over  **C** on  **D** across  **E** by

A   B   C   D   E

**71  was lost ...... the crowd**
    **A** amongst  **B** into  **C** with  **D** through  **E** by

A   B   C   D   E

**72  is proud ...... me**
    **A** with  **B** for  **C** by  **D** of  **E** to

A   B   C   D   E

**73  an exception ...... the rule**
    **A** between  **B** in  **C** to  **D** of  **E** for

A   B   C   D   E

**74  can rely ...... your judgement**
    **A** with  **B** without  **C** before  **D** on  **E** between

A   B   C   D   E

**75  stood ...... the two older boys**
    **A** between  **B** among  **C** for  **D** on  **E** at

A   B   C   D   E

**76  angry ...... the boy who broke the window**
    **A** at  **B** with  **C** over  **D** for  **E** upon

A   B   C   D   E

**77  sat ...... the river and ate his lunch**
    **A** in  **B** on  **C** into  **D** beside  **E** over

A   B   C   D   E

**78  hid ...... the bed to avoid punishment**
    **A** under  **B** above  **C** on  **D** into  **E** around

A   B   C   D   E

**79  arrived ...... the ceremony ended**
    **A** during  **B** before  **C** to  **D** for  **E** at

A   B   C   D   E

Choose the most suitable word to complete each sentence.

80  As we stood and watched a ...... rider appeared in the ring.
    A solitary   B alone   C working   D suddenly
    E soldier

Ⓐ Ⓑ Ⓒ Ⓓ Ⓔ

81  The boxer ...... his title in a well contested fight.
    A defence   B defends   C defended   D defend
    E grabbed

Ⓐ Ⓑ Ⓒ Ⓓ Ⓔ

82  The girl danced ...... and the audience applauded loudly.
    A gloriously   B gracefully   C happy   D crudely
    E clumsily

Ⓐ Ⓑ Ⓒ Ⓓ Ⓔ

83  When the ...... was given, everyone began to move slowly forward.
    A command   B commence   C company
    D camping   E shout

Ⓐ Ⓑ Ⓒ Ⓓ Ⓔ

84  We need to remain ...... if we are to escape.
    A asleep   B awaken   C alert   D happy   E talking

Ⓐ Ⓑ Ⓒ Ⓓ Ⓔ

85  We ...... home as the warning of an approaching hurricane was announced.
    A loitered   B tarried   C hurried   D stopped
    E laughed

Ⓐ Ⓑ Ⓒ Ⓓ Ⓔ

86  John was ...... to take a frog into the class.
    A forbidden   B punished   C angered
    D announced   E reprimanded

Ⓐ Ⓑ Ⓒ Ⓓ Ⓔ

87  You can ...... the one you prefer. I'll have the other.
    A choice   B choose   C chosen   D pick   E chooses

Ⓐ Ⓑ Ⓒ Ⓓ Ⓔ

Choose a word opposite in meaning to the one in capitals.

88  DEFEND
    A play   B attack   C save   D try   E succeed

Ⓐ Ⓑ Ⓒ Ⓓ Ⓔ

89  COWARDLY
    A happy   B bully   C brave   D crowd   E fear

Ⓐ Ⓑ Ⓒ Ⓓ Ⓔ

90  INTERIOR
    A inside   B walls   C afraid   D outside   E within

Ⓐ Ⓑ Ⓒ Ⓓ Ⓔ

9

**91 BROAD**
A big  B wide  C narrow  D long  E large

A  B  C  D  E

**92 CONCISE**
A vague  B confident  C concern  D good  E clear

A  B  C  D  E

**93 CONCEAL**
A advice  B hide  C reveal  D tarry  E tell

A  B  C  D  E

**94 SORROW**
A joy  B sadness  C grief  D sore  E long

A  B  C  D  E

**95 MODERN**
A new  B ancient  C beautiful  D many  E mean

A  B  C  D  E

**96 JUNIOR**
A senior  B boy  C young  D big  E child

A  B  C  D  E

**97 ACCEPT**
A take  B refuse  C glad  D grieve  E gain

A  B  C  D  E

**98 VICTORY**
A defeat  B trouble  C triumph  D games
E players

A  B  C  D  E

**99 COMPLEX**
A difficult  B simple  C building  D complete
E compel

A  B  C  D  E

**100 STALE**
A clean  B good  C fresh  D dirty  E spoilt

A  B  C  D  E

# PAPER TWO

Read the passage carefully then shade in the oval which contains the correct answer to each question.

We are surrounded daily by sounds of all kinds. It is difficult to imagine what it would be like to live in a world without sounds. How sad it would be if we never heard the beautiful sounds of music, the cry of a new-born baby, the song of birds, the buzz of the bees and the happy laughter of children. How strange it would be if we saw the huge waves rushing towards the beach but were unable to hear them splash as the tide ebbed and flowed. And how frightening it would be if we suddenly heard no sound when we spoke.

Some sounds are harsh and unpleasant and we would like to eliminate these from our lives if we could. But the world would be much less exciting and life would be much less pleasant if all sounds were removed, for sounds enable us to communicate with both people and nature.

1  **A world without sound would be**
   **A** strange and unpleasant  **B** exciting
   **C** enjoyed by most people  **D** better for living in
   **E** more relaxing

   Ⓐ  Ⓑ  Ⓒ  Ⓓ  Ⓔ

2  **Eliminate means the same as**
   **A** keep  **B** hear  **C** get rid of  **D** feel  **E** protect

   Ⓐ  Ⓑ  Ⓒ  Ⓓ  Ⓔ

3  **Sounds may be**
   **A** sad  **B** pleasant or unpleasant  **C** loud
   **D** frightening  **E** removed

   Ⓐ  Ⓑ  Ⓒ  Ⓓ  Ⓔ

4  **If we spoke and heard no sound it would be**
   **A** funny  **B** frightening  **C** good  **D** happy
   **E** fortunate

   Ⓐ  Ⓑ  Ⓒ  Ⓓ  Ⓔ

5  **Sounds help us to**
   **A** hear the noise  **B** appreciate man and nature
   **C** enjoy life  **D** be happy  **E** live comfortably

   Ⓐ  Ⓑ  Ⓒ  Ⓓ  Ⓔ

6  **A word opposite in meaning to unpleasant is**
   **A** peaceful  **B** happy  **C** sad  **D** pleasant  **E** unkind

   Ⓐ  Ⓑ  Ⓒ  Ⓓ  Ⓔ

**7** **If we are surrounded by something it is**
 **A** on one side of us   **B** on two sides of us
 **C** all around us   **D** above us   **E** before us

Ⓐ Ⓑ Ⓒ Ⓓ Ⓔ

**8** **Life would be more pleasant if we**
 **A** got rid of all sounds   **B** listened to all sounds
 **C** wore ear plugs   **D** never listened to any sounds
 **E** got rid of harsh sounds

Ⓐ Ⓑ Ⓒ Ⓓ Ⓔ

In each of the following sentences choose the correct spelling for the underlined word.

**9** **The farmer let his cattle into the field to graize on the green grass.**
 **A** gase   **B** graze   **C** gaze   **D** grase   **E** graise

Ⓐ Ⓑ Ⓒ Ⓓ Ⓔ

**10** **The raise of the sun sparkled on the water.**
 **A** raze   **B** rais   **C** rase   **D** rays   **E** raiz

Ⓐ Ⓑ Ⓒ Ⓓ Ⓔ

**11** **The whether was bright and sunny when we set off on our camping trip.**
 **A** weather   **B** wether   **C** wheather   **D** wither
 **E** wuther

Ⓐ Ⓑ Ⓒ Ⓓ Ⓔ

**12** **The sign on the gate clearly said, no admitance.**
 **A** admitence   **B** addmitance   **C** admittance
 **D** admytance   **E** admittence

Ⓐ Ⓑ Ⓒ Ⓓ Ⓔ

**13** **I was decieved by the man posing as my uncle.**
 **A** deceeved   **B** deceaved   **C** deceved   **D** deceived
 **E** deseaved

Ⓐ Ⓑ Ⓒ Ⓓ Ⓔ

**14** **I was most surprised to see Jane at the party in a dress simlar to mine.**
 **A** symilar   **B** seemilar   **C** seamilar   **D** similar
 **E** similer

Ⓐ Ⓑ Ⓒ Ⓓ Ⓔ

**15** **Mary is a very vein girl; she is over conscious about her appearance.**
 **A** vane   **B** veyane   **C** vayain   **D** veane   **E** vain

Ⓐ Ⓑ Ⓒ Ⓓ Ⓔ

**16** **The athletes were proud of their strong mussels.**
 **A** muscles   **B** musels   **C** mussels   **D** muscels
 **E** mussle

Ⓐ Ⓑ Ⓒ Ⓓ Ⓔ

**17** The girl has a very small <u>waste</u>.
   **A** wayste  **B** waist  **C** weighst  **D** waiste  **E** wast

⒜  ⒝  ⒞  ⒟  ⒠

In each of the following sentences choose the form of the word in capitals that correctly completes each one.

**18** **RIDE**  The man ...... a beautiful brown horse.
   **A** ride  **B** riding  **C** ridden  **D** rode  **E** galloped

⒜  ⒝  ⒞  ⒟  ⒠

**19** **LISTEN**  I enjoy talking to Jane who is a keen ......
   She never misses a word you say.
   **A** listens  **B** hears  **C** listened  **D** listening
   **E** listener

⒜  ⒝  ⒞  ⒟  ⒠

**20** **DEPART**  The ...... of the aeroplane was delayed for
   one hour.
   **A** departure  **B** departing  **C** departed  **D** departs
   **E** leaving

⒜  ⒝  ⒞  ⒟  ⒠

**21** **BLOW**  The strong wind ...... the lady's hat off her
   head.
   **A** blow  **B** blowing  **C** blown  **D** blew  **E** pulled

⒜  ⒝  ⒞  ⒟  ⒠

**22** **RING**  The ...... of the bell warned the villagers of
   danger.
   **A** rung  **B** rang  **C** rings  **D** noise  **E** ringing

⒜  ⒝  ⒞  ⒟  ⒠

**23** **IMAGINE**  Jack has a vivid ...... He always makes up
   interesting stories
   **A** imaginary  **B** imagines  **C** imagination
   **D** imagery  **E** imagined

⒜  ⒝  ⒞  ⒟  ⒠

**24** **FORGET**  He has ...... that he should collect his book
   from me.
   **A** forgets  **B** forgotten  **C** forgetting  **D** forgetful
   **E** forgot

⒜  ⒝  ⒞  ⒟  ⒠

**25** **WISE**  He showed much ...... in the decision he made
   to accept the scholarship.
   **A** wisely  **B** wiser  **C** wisdom  **D** sense  **E** thinking

⒜  ⒝  ⒞  ⒟  ⒠

13

In each of the following sentences choose the word that means the same or nearly the same as the word underlined.

26 His grief at the death of his uncle was profound.
   A loss   B sorrow   C gloom   D joy   E hope

   (A)   (B)   (C)   (D)   (E)

27 If our supply of food is depleted before we end our trip we'll be in trouble.
   A spoilt   B sold   C stolen   D lost   E finished

   (A)   (B)   (C)   (D)   (E)

28 We were all astonished when Mary won the contest instead of Ann.
   A amazed   B glad   C sad   D horrified   E pleased

   (A)   (B)   (C)   (D)   (E)

29 The two men debated for hours over the merits of their cars, each claiming his was superior.
   A quarrelled   B laughed   C listened   D argued
   E fought

   (A)   (B)   (C)   (D)   (E)

30 Tom is a very courteous boy. He readily gives his seat to an elderly person.
   A good   B polite   C smart   D quick   E curious

   (A)   (B)   (C)   (D)   (E)

31 I cannot emphasise too strongly the importance of reading instructions carefully in an examination.
   A stress   B say   C tell   D advise   E explain

   (A)   (B)   (C)   (D)   (E)

32 You will not accomplish your ambition unless you begin to work at it now.
   A find   B have   C plan   D achieve   E follow

   (A)   (B)   (C)   (D)   (E)

33 He was stunned when he learnt of the tragic accident.
   A dazed   B pleased   C sad   D glad   E anxious

   (A)   (B)   (C)   (D)   (E)

34 It is difficult to predict what will happen when the principal learns of John's misbehaviour at the match.
   A plan   B see   C pretend   D foretell   E know

   (A)   (B)   (C)   (D)   (E)

35 The job is temporary. It will only last for three weeks.
   A for a short time   B permanent   C for always
   D for a long time   E excellent

   (A)   (B)   (C)   (D)   (E)

36 It is tedious to sit and listen all day without taking part in any activity.
   A interesting   B funny   C easy   D long   E boring

   (A)   (B)   (C)   (D)   (E)

In each of the following choose the word that best completes the phrase.

37  crawled ...... the hedge to get the ball
     **A** by  **B** behind  **C** through  **D** across  **E** around

⒜  Ⓑ  Ⓒ  Ⓓ  Ⓔ

38  jumped ...... the wall to escape the dog
     **A** over  **B** behind  **C** through  **D** from  **E** into

⒜  Ⓑ  Ⓒ  Ⓓ  Ⓔ

39  grateful ...... you for your assistance
     **A** for  **B** to  **C** unto  **D** about  **E** after

⒜  Ⓑ  Ⓒ  Ⓓ  Ⓔ

40  amused ...... his antics
     **A** with  **B** beyond  **C** of  **D** by  **E** over

⒜  Ⓑ  Ⓒ  Ⓓ  Ⓔ

41  must apologise ...... the teacher for his impertinence
     **A** for  **B** to  **C** with  **D** over  **E** before

⒜  Ⓑ  Ⓒ  Ⓓ  Ⓔ

42  heard ...... the train accident late last night
     **A** about  **B** during  **C** before  **D** from  **E** at

⒜  Ⓑ  Ⓒ  Ⓓ  Ⓔ

43  lives ...... the valley
     **A** upon  **B** off  **C** from  **D** beyond  **E** between

⒜  Ⓑ  Ⓒ  Ⓓ  Ⓔ

44  received a letter ...... him today
     **A** by  **B** before  **C** to  **D** without  **E** from

⒜  Ⓑ  Ⓒ  Ⓓ  Ⓔ

Read the following passage carefully, then choose the correct answer to each question.

To our delight, the heavy downpour which began as school was dismissed, flooded the playground behind the school. We liked when it rained after school because as soon as the teachers were gone we would go 'swimming' in the puddles. This was our opportunity to have some fun without being detected, we hoped.

Then on the way home my two friends and I had a grand time for there were puddles all over the road. So we took off our shoes and socks, rolled up our pants and splashed happily along. My sister was much too scared of what mother would do if we got home soaked, so she nimbly avoided the puddles. Needless to say, as we neared home, we were once again properly clad.

**45** **The heavy downpour refers to**
  **A** rain falling   **B** snow storm
  **C** water being poured from a jug   **D** a hurricane
  **E** a tornado

**46** **The boys avoided the teachers because**
  **A** teachers are grouchy
  **B** swimming in the puddles was probably against the rules
  **C** teachers don't like to see children having fun
  **D** teachers do not like boys
  **E** teachers wanted to go swimming too

**47** **A word that means the same as 'opportunity' is**
  **A** time   **B** way   **C** break   **D** chance   **E** belief

**48** **When the boys walked in the puddles they were**
  **A** fully dressed   **B** wearing shirts only   **C** naked
  **D** barefooted   **E** wearing short pants only

**49** **If the boys arrived home wet they would be**
  **A** punished   **B** hugged   **C** given a warm welcome
  **D** polite   **E** receive a treat

**50** **'Properly clad' means the same as**
  **A** avoiding the puddles   **B** being happy
  **C** wearing nothing   **D** fully dressed
  **E** going barefooted

**51** **Rain after school was popular because**
  **A** the afternoons are warmer
  **B** swimming in the puddles would be detected during the day
  **C** afternoons are better for swimming
  **D** rain does not fall in the mornings   **E** boys like rain

**52** **'Scared' means the same as**
  **A** happy   **B** sad   **C** afraid   **D** sure   **E** careful

In each of the following choose the word that is opposite in meaning to the word in capitals.

**53** **REAR**
  **A** back   **B** front   **C** inside   **D** together   **E** outside

**54** **INTERNAL**
  **A** interesting   **B** inside   **C** strong   **D** end
  **E** outside

55 **TAME**
A animal   B pet   C wild   D forest   E tiger

   Ⓐ  Ⓑ  Ⓒ  Ⓓ  Ⓔ

56 **SIMPLE**
A complex   B small   C easy   D problem   E tiny

   Ⓐ  Ⓑ  Ⓒ  Ⓓ  Ⓔ

57 **COMPLETE**
A gain   B win   C show   D sports   E begin

   Ⓐ  Ⓑ  Ⓒ  Ⓓ  Ⓔ

58 **FRIEND**
A kind   B many   C few   D foe   E loyal

   Ⓐ  Ⓑ  Ⓒ  Ⓓ  Ⓔ

59 **EXIT**
A out   B entrance   C in   D leave   E go

   Ⓐ  Ⓑ  Ⓒ  Ⓓ  Ⓔ

60 **ARRIVAL**
A departure   B reach   C come   D go   E airport

   Ⓐ  Ⓑ  Ⓒ  Ⓓ  Ⓔ

61 **EXPORT**
A sell   B buy   C bargain   D import   E market

   Ⓐ  Ⓑ  Ⓒ  Ⓓ  Ⓔ

62 **COARSE**
A rough   B cloth   C fine   D mean   E rude

   Ⓐ  Ⓑ  Ⓒ  Ⓓ  Ⓔ

63 **CONCEAL**
A reveal   B hide   C punish   D steal   E cover

   Ⓐ  Ⓑ  Ⓒ  Ⓓ  Ⓔ

In each of the following sentences the letters ABCDE appear over five words. One is incorrect. Indicate which one by shading the box.

     A  B C D  E
64 The pencil laid on the table.

   Ⓐ  Ⓑ  Ⓒ  Ⓓ  Ⓔ

   A B   C   D     E
65 She is the goodest student in Mathematics.

   Ⓐ  Ⓑ  Ⓒ  Ⓓ  Ⓔ

    A  B    C D   E
66 The man held up the thickest end of the rope.

   Ⓐ  Ⓑ  Ⓒ  Ⓓ  Ⓔ

    A  B  C D   E
67 Everyone have a job for the summer.

   Ⓐ  Ⓑ  Ⓒ  Ⓓ  Ⓔ

  A B C  D E
68 She is taller than me.

   Ⓐ  Ⓑ  Ⓒ  Ⓓ  Ⓔ

17

|  |  | **A B C D  E** | A B C D E |
| --- | --- | --- | --- |
| 69 | The tree had fell across the road. | | Ⓐ Ⓑ Ⓒ Ⓓ Ⓔ |

|  |  | **A  B C    D E** |
| --- | --- | --- |
| 70 | Heavy reigns fell and the roads were flooded. | Ⓐ Ⓑ Ⓒ Ⓓ Ⓔ |

|  |  | **A  B  C D    E** |
| --- | --- | --- |
| 71 | Her brother is bigger than her. | Ⓐ Ⓑ Ⓒ Ⓓ Ⓔ |

|  |  | **A    B  C    D    E** |
| --- | --- | --- |
| 72 | Jane and me saw the children at play. | Ⓐ Ⓑ Ⓒ Ⓓ Ⓔ |

|  |  | **A       B    C  D E** |
| --- | --- | --- |
| 73 | I don't feel well today as I have a soar throat. | Ⓐ Ⓑ Ⓒ Ⓓ Ⓔ |

|  |  | **A  B  C D    E** |
| --- | --- | --- |
| 74 | The letter should have went yesterday. | Ⓐ Ⓑ Ⓒ Ⓓ Ⓔ |

|  |  | **A B    C D E** |
| --- | --- | --- |
| 75 | He begun the book long ago. | Ⓐ Ⓑ Ⓒ Ⓓ Ⓔ |

In each of the following choose the sentence with the best expression.

76   **A** When the speaker was booed, he became angry and shouted at the audience.
    **B** When they boo the speaker they make him angry and he shouted at the audience.
    **C** The speaker was so angry he shouted at the audience when they boo him.
    **D** They booed the speaker and he got angry and shouted at the audience.
    **E** The speaker was mad when he was booed so he shouted at the audience.

                                        Ⓐ Ⓑ Ⓒ Ⓓ Ⓔ

77   **A** The rains so hard all the roads flood and couldn't be passed.
    **B** The impassable roads was because of the flooding by the heavy rains.
    **C** The heavy rains flooded the roads and made them impassable.
    **D** The roads flooded by the heavy rains were impassable.
    **E** The heavy rains flooded the roads and you couldn't pass.

                                        Ⓐ Ⓑ Ⓒ Ⓓ Ⓔ

**78**
A Because of the long drought the plants them just wither up and died.
B The plants wither and die because of the long drought.
C Because the drought was so long many plants just wither up and died.
D The long drought made the plants wither and die.
E Because of the long drought many plants withered and died.

Ⓐ Ⓑ Ⓒ Ⓓ Ⓔ

**79**
A The happy children laughed in the air.
B As the children played, their happy laughter filled the air.
C The children laughed hard when they played.
D The happy laughter of playing children filled the air.
E The air was full of happy laughter as the children played.

Ⓐ Ⓑ Ⓒ Ⓓ Ⓔ

**80**
A Children usually have lots of fun in the holidays.
B School holidays is a time full of fun for children.
C Children have much fun during holidays away from school.
D School holidays are full of fun for children.
E School holidays can be much fun usually for children.

Ⓐ Ⓑ Ⓒ Ⓓ Ⓔ

In each of the following choose the word which means the same or nearly the same as the word in capitals.

**81 BENIGN**
A attractive  B kind  C careful  D quiet
E disobliging

Ⓐ Ⓑ Ⓒ Ⓓ Ⓔ

**82 LIVELY**
A active  B dull  C weak  D happy  E quiet

Ⓐ Ⓑ Ⓒ Ⓓ Ⓔ

**83 ESTABLISHED**
A destroyed  B made  C founded  D performed
E easy

Ⓐ Ⓑ Ⓒ Ⓓ Ⓔ

**84 DEFACE**
A improve  B clean  C preserve  D disfigure
E decay

Ⓐ Ⓑ Ⓒ Ⓓ Ⓔ

**85 CONSTRUCT**
A house  B destroy  C raze  D strengthen  E build

Ⓐ Ⓑ Ⓒ Ⓓ Ⓔ

**86 FORGIVE**
   A pardon   B plead   C beg   D blame   E censure

   Ⓐ Ⓑ Ⓒ Ⓓ Ⓔ

**87 PENITENT**
   A patience   B pride   C crime   D reward
   E sorrowful

   Ⓐ Ⓑ Ⓒ Ⓓ Ⓔ

**88 SCARCE**
   A insufficient   B enough   C sufficient   D hard
   E find

   Ⓐ Ⓑ Ⓒ Ⓓ Ⓔ

**89 QUEER**
   A normal   B bad   C odd   D rare   E quick

   Ⓐ Ⓑ Ⓒ Ⓓ Ⓔ

**90 ALERT**
   A slow   B vigilant   C furious   D listless   E scared

   Ⓐ Ⓑ Ⓒ Ⓓ Ⓔ

**91 ACCURATE**
   A correct   B swift   C accused   D inaccurate
   E wrong

   Ⓐ Ⓑ Ⓒ Ⓓ Ⓔ

**92 COMMAND**
   A beseech   B officer   C march   D order   E dismiss

   Ⓐ Ⓑ Ⓒ Ⓓ Ⓔ

In each of the following sentences choose the word that
correctly completes each sentence.

**93 The little girl ...... the candy offered by the stranger.**
   A released   B refused   C reduced   D read
   E recalled

   Ⓐ Ⓑ Ⓒ Ⓓ Ⓔ

**94 James is very ...... He spends his money carefully.**
   A thrilled   B strong   C greedy   D thrifty
   E terrible

   Ⓐ Ⓑ Ⓒ Ⓓ Ⓔ

**95 Non-swimmers should stay out of the ...... end of the
pool.**
   A depth   B narrow   C deep   D clean   E shallow

   Ⓐ Ⓑ Ⓒ Ⓓ Ⓔ

**96 When sugar is ...... everyone tries to hoard it.**
   A plentiful   B sweet   C brown   D refined   E scarce

   Ⓐ Ⓑ Ⓒ Ⓓ Ⓔ

**97 We watched the ...... of the President on television.**
   A arrive   B arrival   C arising   D attention
   E ardour

   Ⓐ Ⓑ Ⓒ Ⓓ Ⓔ

**98** The man was found ...... and sentenced to jail for a
year.
A innocent   B good   C guilty   D crazy   E hiding

Ⓐ   Ⓑ   Ⓒ   Ⓓ   Ⓔ

**99** The meeting ...... with the singing of a hymn.
A commenced   B comforted   C came   D called
E communed

Ⓐ   Ⓑ   Ⓒ   Ⓓ   Ⓔ

**100** The ...... was hot and so we spent many days on the
beach.
A whether   B wind   C weather   D weird   E rain

Ⓐ   Ⓑ   Ⓒ   Ⓓ   Ⓔ

# PAPER THREE

Read each of the following sentences carefully then choose the word that correctly completes each of the sentences.

1 The boy complained that he had not ...... his birthday gift from his grandmother.
   A obtained  B dismissed  C received  D sent
   E returned
   Ⓐ Ⓑ Ⓒ Ⓓ Ⓔ

2 The manager handed his ...... the letter to be typed.
   A servant  B electrician  C secretary  D gardener
   E opponent
   Ⓐ Ⓑ Ⓒ Ⓓ Ⓔ

3 The judge ...... the prisoner to death.
   A freed  B condemned  C released  D employed
   E sacrificed
   Ⓐ Ⓑ Ⓒ Ⓓ Ⓔ

4 The opening of ...... is always an historic occasion.
   A Parliament  B audience  C games  D library
   E school
   Ⓐ Ⓑ Ⓒ Ⓓ Ⓔ

5 The garden was fragrant with the scent of the blooming ......
   A animals  B flowers  C stones  D grass  E crotons
   Ⓐ Ⓑ Ⓒ Ⓓ Ⓔ

6 At last I reached the ...... and was able to pay for my items.
   A dentist  B cashier  C higgler  D telephonist
   E teller
   Ⓐ Ⓑ Ⓒ Ⓓ Ⓔ

7 The two parties ...... the issue for many hours.
   A debated  B wedded  C memorised  D sang
   E raged
   Ⓐ Ⓑ Ⓒ Ⓓ Ⓔ

8 The driver failed to stop at the ...... sign.
   A traffic  B riding  C vehicle  D walking
   E moving
   Ⓐ Ⓑ Ⓒ Ⓓ Ⓔ

9 An eagle lives in an ......
   A aviary  B igloo  C eyrie  D apiary  E convent
   Ⓐ Ⓑ Ⓒ Ⓓ Ⓔ

10 A synonym for humble is ......
   A poor  B humility  C pious  D adverse
   E good
   Ⓐ Ⓑ Ⓒ Ⓓ Ⓔ

22

Read the following sentences then select the correct form.

11 A  Between you and I they are both guilty.
   B  Between you and me they are both guilty.
   C  Between you and him they are both guilty.
   D  You and me between us knows they are guilty.
   E  Between me and you they are both guilty.

    (A)   (B)   (C)   (D)   (E)

12 A  Mary is the tallest of the two children.
   B  Mary is the taller of the two children.
   C  Mary is the tallest of the child.
   D  Mary is tall of the children.
   E  Mary is the taller of the child.

    (A)   (B)   (C)   (D)   (E)

13 A  Each of the girls have a pen.
   B  Each of the girls has a pen.
   C  Each of the girl has a pen.
   D  Each of the girls have a pens.
   E  Each of the girl have a pen.

    (A)   (B)   (C)   (D)   (E)

14 A  The conductor, with several others, was late.
   B  The conductor, with several others, were late.
   C  The conductor, with several other was late.
   D  The conductor, with several other were late.
   E  The conductors, with several others, was late.

    (A)   (B)   (C)   (D)   (E)

15 A  John, as well as Donald, are clever.
   B  John, as well as Donald, is clever.
   C  John, as well as Donald, were clever.
   D  John, as well as Donald have been clever.
   E  John, as well as Donald am clever.

    (A)   (B)   (C)   (D)   (E)

In each of the following sentences choose the word that gives the correct part of speech of the one underlined, as used in each sentence.

16 **Jerry is a famous magician.**
   A  noun   B  preposition   C  adverb   D  interjection
   E  adjective

    (A)   (B)   (C)   (D)   (E)

17 **Mother prepared an excellent meal.**
   A  pronoun   B  preposition   C  conjunction
   D  adverb   E  noun

    (A)   (B)   (C)   (D)   (E)

**18** Kay has been a successful <u>law</u> student.
   **A** noun   **B** adverb   **C** adjective   **D** conjunction
   **E** pronoun

Ⓐ Ⓑ Ⓒ Ⓓ Ⓔ

**19** <u>Are you going</u> to give it to her?
   **A** adverb   **B** verb   **C** noun   **D** preposition
   **E** pronoun

Ⓐ Ⓑ Ⓒ Ⓓ Ⓔ

**20** 'Come <u>to</u> me,' said the man.
   **A** noun   **B** pronoun   **C** adverb   **D** adjective
   **E** preposition

Ⓐ Ⓑ Ⓒ Ⓓ Ⓔ

**21** He discovered Neville <u>and</u> Kingsley hiding behind the
   tree.
   **A** noun   **B** conjunction   **C** preposition   **D** verb
   **E** adverb

Ⓐ Ⓑ Ⓒ Ⓓ Ⓔ

**22** <u>Suddenly</u> a loud rumbling was heard.
   **A** verb   **B** pronoun   **C** conjunction   **D** adjective
   **E** adverb

Ⓐ Ⓑ Ⓒ Ⓓ Ⓔ

**23** I gave <u>it</u> to him.
   **A** pronoun   **B** adjective   **C** adverb   **D** preposition
   **E** conjunction

Ⓐ Ⓑ Ⓒ Ⓓ Ⓔ

Read the passage carefully then choose the correct answer to
each question.

Looking at the young woman, Tony was immediately struck
by her amazing beauty. She was a fragile creature with tiny
white teeth and short curly black hair. His eyes followed as she
walked towards the building. Suddenly she turned and met the
eyes of her admirer.

**24** Fragile is the opposite of ......
   **A** delicate   **B** easily broken   **C** hard   **D** brittle
   **E** robust

Ⓐ Ⓑ Ⓒ Ⓓ Ⓔ

**25** The word which means the same as tiny is ......
   **A** gigantic   **B** huge   **C** large   **D** small   **E** enormous

Ⓐ Ⓑ Ⓒ Ⓓ Ⓔ

**26** In the passage the word which means the same as
   'amazing' is ......
   **A** hated   **B** sudden   **C** immediate   **D** admired
   **E** unbelievable

Ⓐ Ⓑ Ⓒ Ⓓ Ⓔ

27 **Why was Tony looking at the young woman?**
   **A** she was very beautiful   **B** he did not like her
   **C** she talked too much   **D** she was a strange creature
   **E** she was ugly

28 **How would you describe the girl's hair?**
   **A** straight   **B** dark brown   **C** curly
   **D** straight and black   **E** curly and black

29 **'His eyes followed her' means ......**
   **A** his eyes walked after her   **B** his eyes popped out
   **C** he gazed after her   **D** he looked at her
   **E** he glanced in her direction

30 **From the passage you could conclude that the young man ......**
   **A** was attracted by her beauty   **B** hated her
   **C** was disappointed in what he saw
   **D** noticed her beautiful voice   **E** was angry with her

In each of the following choose the word that correctly completes each sentence.

31 **The chairman ...... at the electrician yesterday.**
   **A** shout   **B** shouts   **C** was shouted   **D** shouted
   **E** shouting

32 **'I will be late tonight, Mom,' Sally ......**
   **A** indicate   **B** answered   **C** indicated   **D** answer
   **E** indicates

33 **The ...... seemed a little confused.**
   **A** administer   **B** administrating   **C** administrator
   **D** administrates   **E** administrated

34 **An ...... is a division of a play.**
   **A** action   **B** actor   **C** act   **D** activity   **E** acts

35 **To activate is to ......**
   **A** put down   **B** stimulate   **C** act   **D** reactivate
   **E** stop

36 **He is ...... to arrive tonight.**
   **A** expected   **B** anticipated   **C** about   **D** schedule
   **E** suppose

25

In each sentence one word is wrongly spelt. Choose the correct spelling for the underlined word.

37  The Prime Minister's speech was very <u>disticnt</u>.
A dysticnt   B distinct   C disinct   D destinct
E dystincts

ⓐ  ⓑ  ⓒ  ⓓ  ⓔ

38  Doctors are often very <u>patience</u> individuals.
A pateince   B patients   C patient   D pateints
E pateeince

ⓐ  ⓑ  ⓒ  ⓓ  ⓔ

39  Children are encouraged to be <u>poliet</u>
A polight   B polite   C polyte   D polighte   E pulite

ⓐ  ⓑ  ⓒ  ⓓ  ⓔ

40  Sarah blushed at his <u>complement</u>.
A complyment   B compliment   C complemient
D complment   E compleement

ⓐ  ⓑ  ⓒ  ⓓ  ⓔ

41  Cholera is an infectious <u>dicease</u>.
A decease   B disease   C dizease   D dissease
E desease

ⓐ  ⓑ  ⓒ  ⓓ  ⓔ

42  The teacher's attempt to stop the blood was in <u>vane</u>.
A vein   B vain   C vayne   D vaine   E veine

ⓐ  ⓑ  ⓒ  ⓓ  ⓔ

43  Her mother gave her a beautiful <u>bruch</u>.
A brooch   B broach   C browch   D bruche
E broache

ⓐ  ⓑ  ⓒ  ⓓ  ⓔ

44  Jonathan gave me a packet of <u>currents</u>.
A curants   B curents   C currants   D carrents
E currencts

ⓐ  ⓑ  ⓒ  ⓓ  ⓔ

45  His present was attractive but too expensive for me to <u>acept</u>.
A aceppt   B except   C accept   D axcept   E accepte

ⓐ  ⓑ  ⓒ  ⓓ  ⓔ

46  The sack was made of <u>coorse</u> material.
A course   B coarse   C corse   D cospe   E cawrse

ⓐ  ⓑ  ⓒ  ⓓ  ⓔ

47  His <u>berth</u> was a joyful occasion.
A birth   B burth   C birthe   D berthe   E brith

ⓐ  ⓑ  ⓒ  ⓓ  ⓔ

48  She spoke with a French <u>assent</u>.
A accent   B ascent   C axcent   D acent   E ascente

ⓐ  ⓑ  ⓒ  ⓓ  ⓔ

**49**   **The scientist is considered a <u>genuic</u>.**
     **A** geenus   **B** genuis   **C** geneus   **D** genius   **E** jenius

Ⓐ   Ⓑ   Ⓒ   Ⓓ   Ⓔ

**50**   **There were sounds of <u>gaeety</u> and laughter everywhere.**
     **A** gayity   **B** gaieti   **C** gaiety   **D** gaeti   **E** gayiety

Ⓐ   Ⓑ   Ⓒ   Ⓓ   Ⓔ

Choose the sentence which is correctly punctuated.

**51**   **A**  The boy bought, sweets peanuts and cake.
     **B**  The boy bought sweets peanuts and cake.
     **C**  The boy bought sweets peanuts, and cake
     **D**  The boy bought sweets, peanuts and cake.
     **E**  The boy bought sweets peanuts, and cake.

Ⓐ   Ⓑ   Ⓒ   Ⓓ   Ⓔ

**52**   **A**  I will not be going to the movie,
     **B**  I will not be going to the movie.
     **C**  I will, not be going, to the movie.
     **D**  I will not be going, to the movie.
     **E**  I will not be going to; the movie.

Ⓐ   Ⓑ   Ⓒ   Ⓓ   Ⓔ

**53**   **A**  'Don't do that Ricky, you will hurt yourself.
     **B**  Dont do that Ricky you will hurt yourself.'
     **C**  'Dont do that Ricky.' 'You will hurt yourself.'
     **D**  Don't do that ricky, 'you will hurt yourself.
     **E**  'Don't do that Ricky! You will hurt yourself.'

Ⓐ   Ⓑ   Ⓒ   Ⓓ   Ⓔ

**54**   **A**  'Would you come with me?' asked Toni.
     **B**  Would you come with me? asked Toni.
     **C**  'Would you come with me? asked Toni.
     **D**  'Would you come with me' asked Toni
     **E**  'Would you come with me?' asked Toni,

Ⓐ   Ⓑ   Ⓒ   Ⓓ   Ⓔ

**55**   **A**  Are you going tomorrow
     **B**  are you going tomorrow?
     **C**  Are you going, tomorrow
     **D**  Are you going tomorrow?
     **E**  Are you going tomorrow!

Ⓐ   Ⓑ   Ⓒ   Ⓓ   Ⓔ

In each of the following choose the word that will make the passage correct when completed.

**56**   **I am going to look …… the door, to see if I can find the broom.**
     **A** in front of   **B** in   **C** behind   **D** inside
     **E** underneath

Ⓐ   Ⓑ   Ⓒ   Ⓓ   Ⓔ

**57** 'It is not there,' Tony said. 'I was looking ...... it.'
  **A** at  **B** for  **C** near  **D** in  **E** next to

 Ⓐ Ⓑ Ⓒ Ⓓ Ⓔ

**58** Then it must be ...... Mrs Morgan's room.
  **A** in  **B** from  **C** next to  **D** interior  **E** into

 Ⓐ Ⓑ Ⓒ Ⓓ Ⓔ

**59** 'It is not there either, I looked ......'
  **A** always  **B** over  **C** everywhere  **D** into  **E** from

 Ⓐ Ⓑ Ⓒ Ⓓ Ⓔ

**60** You will have to borrow one ...... Mrs Ward.
  **A** at  **B** nearby  **C** in  **D** from  **E** underneath

 Ⓐ Ⓑ Ⓒ Ⓓ Ⓔ

Choose the word which is the opposite of the underlined word.

**61** Smoking is <u>prohibited</u> in school.
  **A** permit  **B** disallowed  **C** permitted  **D** done
  **E** grant

 Ⓐ Ⓑ Ⓒ Ⓓ Ⓕ

**62** A <u>miniature</u> statue was placed by the entrance.
  **A** small  **B** tiny  **C** enormous  **D** grand  **E** little

 Ⓐ Ⓑ Ⓒ Ⓓ Ⓔ

**63** The aircraft was now <u>visible</u>.
  **A** discernible  **B** beyond the clouds  **C** out of sight
  **D** hardly seen  **E** in view

 Ⓐ Ⓑ Ⓒ Ⓓ Ⓔ

**64** The toy was completely <u>immersed in water</u>.
  **A** under the water  **B** partly under water
  **C** out of the water  **D** wet  **E** underneath

 Ⓐ Ⓑ Ⓒ Ⓓ Ⓔ

**65** The sums were very <u>simple</u>.
  **A** easy  **B** poor  **C** difficult  **D** slight  **E** little

 Ⓐ Ⓑ Ⓒ Ⓓ Ⓔ

**66** It is <u>illegal</u> to drive without a licence.
  **A** legal  **B** not good  **C** right  **D** not right
  **E** excellent

 Ⓐ Ⓑ Ⓒ Ⓓ Ⓔ

**67** The climate was <u>unpleasant</u>.
  **A** rainy  **B** unkind  **C** unhealthy  **D** dry
  **E** pleasant

 Ⓐ Ⓑ Ⓒ Ⓓ Ⓔ

**68** She was <u>crying</u> because she got a beautiful present.
  **A** laughing  **B** gay  **C** light hearted  **D** miserable
  **E** sprightly

 Ⓐ Ⓑ Ⓒ Ⓓ Ⓔ

**69** The chairs were <u>hard</u> and uncomfortable.
  **A** soft  **B** easy  **C** simple  **D** pretty  **E** light

 Ⓐ Ⓑ Ⓒ Ⓓ Ⓔ

**70**  **Regular visits were made to the doctor.**
  **A** often  **B** irregular  **C** scarcely  **D** intermittently
  **E** once in a while

A   B   C   D   E

In each of the following choose the word that means the same as the underlined words.

**71**  **There was a <u>hive of bees</u> in the tree.**
  **A** swarm  **B** flock  **C** school  **D** group  **E** many

A   B   C   D   E

**72**  **A <u>group of herrings</u> was found in the warm water.**
  **A** shoal  **B** flock  **C** herd  **D** litter  **E** hive

A   B   C   D   E

**73**  **The cat gave birth to a <u>number</u> of kittens.**
  **A** brood  **B** litter  **C** swarm  **D** school  **E** flock

A   B   C   D   E

**74**  **The <u>people in the church</u> listened intently to the sermon.**
  **A** audience  **B** mob  **C** crowd  **D** congregation
  **E** students

A   B   C   D   E

**75**  **Having finished with the buns, the baker placed <u>some loaves</u> of bread in the oven.**
  **A** a shoal  **B** a school  **C** a flock  **D** an amount
  **E** a batch

A   B   C   D   E

Read the following passage carefully then choose the correct answer to each question.

The little village of Williamsfield, in Jamaica, was bustling with activity. News had arrived that Edward Sims and his wife and two children were arriving the next day from England.

Kingsley watched all the preparations with excitement. While he had heard of Uncle Edward and Aunt Clare, he had no recollection of their appearance. Even worse, he had no idea of what his cousins Sarah and Nehemiah Sims looked like. This was not surprising since they were born in Manchester, England.

He imagined they would look white since all the English people he had met were white and spoke with a strange accent.

One can therefore appreciate his shock when the car stopped and the black couple emerged with a boy and girl looking just like him.

**76** Why was there excitement in the village of Williamsfield?
**A** Something disastrous happened the evening before.
**B** News arrived.
**C** Uncle Edward and his family were arriving the next day.
**D** There was a car accident.
**E** The next day was visitors' day.

(A) (B) (C) (D) (E)

**77** In the passage another word for 'excitement' could be
**A** agitation **B** belief **C** amazement **D** surprise
**E** disenchantment

(A) (B) (C) (D) (E)

**78** From the passage one can assume that Sarah and Nehemiah Sims were
**A** black **B** Chinese **C** white **D** American
**E** timid

(A) (B) (C) (D) (E)

**79** The word 'emerged' means the same as
**A** went away **B** departed **C** came out
**D** embarked **E** entered

(A) (B) (C) (D) (E)

**80** From which country did Sarah and Nehemiah come?
**A** Barbados **B** Jamaica **C** England **D** U.S.A.
**E** Williamsfield

(A) (B) (C) (D) (E)

**81** The opposite of 'recollect' is
**A** remembrance **B** forget **C** thought
**D** revelation **E** disclosure

(A) (B) (C) (D) (E)

Choose the word which could be used instead of the one underlined.

**82** The teacher stopped the boys from playing with the bamboo sticks.
**A** prevented **B** allowed **C** encouraged **D** ended
**E** removed

(A) (B) (C) (D) (E)

**83** She met a boy in ragged apparel.
**A** look **B** clothes **C** sight **D** appearance **E** shape

(A) (B) (C) (D) (E)

**84** These sentences should be omitted from the report.
**A** given **B** retained **C** joined **D** dropped
**E** added

(A) (B) (C) (D) (E)

85  **Do you remember having lost this pencil?**
    **A** recall  **B** express  **C** shout  **D** forget  **E** receipt

    (A)  (B)  (C)  (D)  (E)

86  **My car has several defective parts.**
    **A** faulty  **B** correct  **C** effective  **D** noisy  **E** wrong

    (A)  (B)  (C)  (D)  (E)

87  **The teacher saw herself as a lady of some distinction.**
    **A** carried  **B** termed  **C** described  **D** visualized
    **E** timed

    (A)  (B)  (C)  (D)  (E)

88  **The boy was suspended from school because of his crude behaviour.**
    **A** wicked  **B** rough  **C** quick  **D** big  **E** simple

    (A)  (B)  (C)  (D)  (E)

89  **Her anger was uncontrollable.**
    **A** fury  **B** future  **C** distress  **D** stillness  **E** anxiety

    (A)  (B)  (C)  (D)  (E)

90  **My father wastes much time on trivial matters.**
    **A** unimportant  **B** important  **C** difficult  **D** small
    **E** mean

    (A)  (B)  (C)  (D)  (E)

91  **It is customary for turtles to lay their eggs in the sand.**
    **A** considerate  **B** difficult  **C** unusual  **D** good
    **E** usual

    (A)  (B)  (C)  (D)  (E)

92  **The child is stubborn and will not do as he is told.**
    **A** willing  **B** strong  **C** unrepentant  **D** tough
    **E** obstinate

    (A)  (B)  (C)  (D)  (E)

93  **The windows were made of transparent glass.**
    **A** opaque  **B** clear  **C** black  **D** translucent
    **E** permanent

    (A)  (B)  (C)  (D)  (E)

94  **The imposter cheated the lady and collected her rent.**
    **A** received  **B** tolerated  **C** despised  **D** loved
    **E** deceived

    (A)  (B)  (C)  (D)  (E)

95  **The destruction caused by the hurricane was a calamity.**
    **A** danger  **B** outstanding  **C** disaster
    **D** celebration  **E** event

    (A)  (B)  (C)  (D)  (E)

96  **The constable arrived as the robbers were leaving.**
    **A** policeman  **B** soldier  **C** doctor  **D** nurse
    **E** sailor

    (A)  (B)  (C)  (D)  (E)

Choose the correct sentence.

**97**  **A** The salesman from the furniture store arrived with the tables.
    **B** The salesman arrived with the tables to the furniture store.
    **C** The salesman arrived to the store with the tables from the furniture store.
    **D** The salesman arrives with the tables from the furniture store.
    **E** The salesman were arriving with the tables from the furniture store.

Ⓐ  Ⓑ  Ⓒ  Ⓓ  Ⓔ

**98**  **A** She have ten children
    **B** She has ten children.
    **C** She have been having ten children.
    **D** She haves ten children.
    **E** She is having ten children.

Ⓐ  Ⓑ  Ⓒ  Ⓓ  Ⓔ

**99**  **A** He did go last night.
    **B** He is going last night.
    **C** He went last night.
    **D** He had been going last night.
    **E** He were going last night.

Ⓐ  Ⓑ  Ⓒ  Ⓓ  Ⓔ

**100**  **A** The market seller were having mangoes.
    **B** The market seller had mangoes.
    **C** The market seller was having mangoes.
    **D** The market seller have been having mangoes.
    **E** The market seller has been having mangoes.

Ⓐ  Ⓑ  Ⓒ  Ⓓ  Ⓔ

# PAPER FOUR

Read the passage carefully then answer the questions by choosing the word which correctly completes each of the sentences.

The darkness has dispersed and the day dawns bright and clear. There is the clean fresh smell of the morning air, the grass is wet with dew and man is at peace with himself and the world. Then the sun rises, the hustle and bustle of the day begins and this beautiful peace is shattered.

1  **The morning air is**
   **A** polluted  **B** cold  **C** fresh  **D** wet  **E** dry

   Ⓐ  Ⓑ  Ⓒ  Ⓓ  Ⓔ

2  **Dawn is**
   **A** before sunrise  **B** after sunrise  **C** mid-day
   **D** noon  **E** evening

   Ⓐ  Ⓑ  Ⓒ  Ⓓ  Ⓔ

3  **'Dispersed' means the same as**
   **A** displeased  **B** happened  **C** disappeared  **D** come
   **E** fallen

   Ⓐ  Ⓑ  Ⓒ  Ⓓ  Ⓔ

4  **The grass is wet because**
   **A** it has rained  **B** dew has formed
   **C** the air is cool  **D** it is morning
   **E** the sun has not yet risen

   Ⓐ  Ⓑ  Ⓒ  Ⓓ  Ⓔ

5  **After sunrise the peace is destroyed because**
   **A** the sunrise shatters it  **B** the day's activities begin
   **C** man is angry  **D** everyone is asleep
   **E** the sun gets hot

   Ⓐ  Ⓑ  Ⓒ  Ⓓ  Ⓔ

6  **The writer likes this time of day because**
   **A** it is dark  **B** it is cool  **C** the sun has not yet risen
   **D** it is peaceful  **E** it is noisy

   Ⓐ  Ⓑ  Ⓒ  Ⓓ  Ⓔ

In each of the following choose the word which means the same as the word underlined.

7  **Christopher Columbus discovered Jamaica.**
   **A** bought  **B** found  **C** lost  **D** sold  **E** claimed

   Ⓐ  Ⓑ  Ⓒ  Ⓓ  Ⓔ

**8** We will now <u>conclude</u> our discussions until we meet again.

   **A** begin  **B** start  **C** commence  **D** end  **E** confide

      (A)  (B)  (C)  (D)  (E)

**9** Are you able to <u>comprehend</u> such a difficult book?

   **A** read  **B** understand  **C** borrow  **D** buy  **E** use

      (A)  (B)  (C)  (D)  (E)

**10** You are a <u>fortunate</u> child, you have parents who really care about you.

   **A** good  **B** happy  **C** favourite  **D** kind  **E** lucky

      (A)  (B)  (C)  (D)  (E)

**11** The boy was punished for his <u>insolent</u> behaviour.

   **A** polite  **B** discreet  **C** impertinent  **D** unkind  **E** proud

      (A)  (B)  (C)  (D)  (E)

**12** You should not worry over such <u>trivial</u> things which do not really matter.

   **A** small  **B** bad  **C** funny  **D** important  **E** sacred

      (A)  (B)  (C)  (D)  (E)

**13** Mary is a very <u>timid</u> girl, she spoke to no one at the party.

   **A** proud  **B** pretty  **C** fat  **D** shy  **E** big

      (A)  (B)  (C)  (D)  (E)

**14** Please <u>indicate</u> your agreement by raising your hand.

   **A** turn  **B** show  **C** say  **D** tell  **E** prepare

      (A)  (B)  (C)  (D)  (E)

**15** The land was bare and <u>arid</u>, only cactus grew there.

   **A** hot  **B** wet  **C** rich  **D** pasture  **E** dry

      (A)  (B)  (C)  (D)  (E)

**16** It is hard to <u>predict</u> how she will react when she hears the news.

   **A** foretell  **B** know  **C** believe  **D** argue  **E** say

      (A)  (B)  (C)  (D)  (E)

**17** The house on the corner has been <u>vacant</u> since the family moved out.

   **A** big  **B** painted  **C** empty  **D** cleaned  **E** sold

      (A)  (B)  (C)  (D)  (E)

**18** Can you <u>recall</u> what his address was?

   **A** write  **B** read  **C** tell  **D** remember  **E** see

      (A)  (B)  (C)  (D)  (E)

In each of the following sentences find the correct spelling of the word underlined.

**19** Did you see the funny <u>cartons</u> in the paper?

   **A** kartones  **B** cartoons  **C** kartoons  **D** cartones  **E** cartunes

      (A)  (B)  (C)  (D)  (E)

**20** The tree was struck by <u>lightening</u> during the thunder-storm.
**A** lightning    **B** litenining    **C** lighting    **D** lytening
**E** lightenying

   (A)  (B)  (C)  (D)  (E)

**21** We were <u>adviced</u> to drive carefully as the road became slippery when wet.
**A** advyced    **B** adviesed    **C** addvised    **D** advised
**E** addviced

   (A)  (B)  (C)  (D)  (E)

**22** The old woman sat by the window <u>nitting</u> a red sweater.
**A** kniting    **B** nytting    **C** knitting    **D** knytting
**E** niting

   (A)  (B)  (C)  (D)  (E)

**23** The strong wind <u>blue</u> the woman's hat off her head.
**A** blow    **B** blew    **C** bleu    **D** blieu    **E** bloo

   (A)  (B)  (C)  (D)  (E)

**24** A <u>quare</u> old man sat by the fireside.
**A** quere    **B** quear    **C** queer    **D** quaire    **E** quair

   (A)  (B)  (C)  (D)  (E)

**25** The girl is suffering from a rare <u>dezees</u>.
**A** deseez    **B** dezeez    **C** disease    **D** desease
**E** dezease

   (A)  (B)  (C)  (D)  (E)

**26** Did you <u>beleave</u> the story he told?
**A** believe    **B** bileave    **C** beleive    **D** beleeve
**E** beleve

   (A)  (B)  (C)  (D)  (E)

**27** Mr Jones was involved in an <u>axedent</u> last week.
**A** acident    **B** accident    **C** axident    **D** askident
**E** actsident

   (A)  (B)  (C)  (D)  (E)

**28** He used <u>ceiling</u> wax to stick down the stamp.
**A** ceeling    **B** sealing    **C** seiling    **D** cealing
**E** seeling

   (A)  (B)  (C)  (D)  (E)

**29** The man used <u>bored</u> to make the desks and chairs.
**A** boored    **B** boared    **C** board    **D** boad    **E** boryd

   (A)  (B)  (C)  (D)  (E)

**30** Joan <u>dose</u> not go to the same school as Mary.
**A** doze    **B** doez    **C** doose    **D** does    **E** dooze

   (A)  (B)  (C)  (D)  (E)

In each of the following sentences choose the form of the word in capitals which correctly completes each sentence.

31  **ALLOW**   He spent his week's …… at once and so had no money left.
A allowed   B allows   C allowance   D allowing
E disallow
Ⓐ Ⓑ Ⓒ Ⓓ Ⓔ

32  **ATTEND**   He …… the same high school as my brother.
A attends   B attendance   C attending   D attention
E attentive
Ⓐ Ⓑ Ⓒ Ⓓ Ⓔ

33  **REBEL**   The ……. began when one of the workers was killed in an explosion at the factory.
A rebels   B rebellion   C rebelling   D rebelled
E destruction
Ⓐ Ⓑ Ⓒ Ⓓ Ⓔ

34  **BEG**   I feel sorry for the poor …… who sits at the corner every day asking for food.
A begs   B begging   C beggar   D begged   E begger
Ⓐ Ⓑ Ⓒ Ⓓ Ⓔ

35  **INJURE**   His …… were not as serious as we had thought.
A injured   B injuries   C injury   D cuts   E bruises
Ⓐ Ⓑ Ⓒ Ⓓ Ⓔ

36  **DISCOVER**   The …… of oil on Mr Brown's land caused great excitement among the neighbours.
A discovered   B discovers   C discovering
D discovery   E finding
Ⓐ Ⓑ Ⓒ Ⓓ Ⓔ

37  **CARE**   Her …… attitude made me realise she meant well even though I was in pain.
A careful   B cares   C cared   D careth   E caring
Ⓐ Ⓑ Ⓒ Ⓓ Ⓔ

38  **PROUD**   She took great …… in her work and was rewarded with good grades in class.
A pride   B proudly   C prided   D prides   E boast
Ⓐ Ⓑ Ⓒ Ⓓ Ⓔ

39  **LISTEN**   The audience …… attentively to the guest speaker at the prize-giving last week.
A listens   B listening   C listener   D listened
E heard
Ⓐ Ⓑ Ⓒ Ⓓ Ⓔ

40  **HIGH**   The …… of the tree was fifty feet.
A height   B highness   C highs   D highten
E hightening
Ⓐ Ⓑ Ⓒ Ⓓ Ⓔ

**41  BOY**   In his ……, my father was an excellent football player.
A  boys   B  boyish   C  boyhood   D  childhood
E  infancy

Ⓐ  Ⓑ  Ⓒ  Ⓓ  Ⓔ

**42  COME**   They …… to school early this morning.
A  comes   B  came   C  coming   D  become   E  income

Ⓐ  Ⓑ  Ⓒ  Ⓓ  Ⓔ

Read the following passage carefully, then choose the correct answer.

The house, which stood a little distance from the road, looked deserted and the tree laden with red apples very tempting. Tom and Joe debated whether they should climb the high wall and attempt to get some of the luscious-looking apples. Yes, they couldn't resist it. Those apples looked just too good. So over the wall they went and stealthily approached the tree. Quickly Tom clambered up and was soon dropping apples into the eager waiting hands of Joe. Then around the corner of the house a well-dressed man appeared. Joe 'froze', and Tom, unaware of the danger, called, 'Hey Joe, catch!' The man, hearing the sound, looked around and went towards the tree.

**43  The boys went to pick the apples because they thought**
A  that no one lived at the house
B  apples were good food
C  they were given permission to pick them
D  the apples were red   E  they thought it was fun

Ⓐ  Ⓑ  Ⓒ  Ⓓ  Ⓔ

**44  To get the apples Tom**
A  stood on the ground   B  climbed the tree
C  threw stones   D  used a stick   E  used a ladder

Ⓐ  Ⓑ  Ⓒ  Ⓓ  Ⓔ

**45  'Debated' means the same as**
A  fussed   B  agreed   C  angered   D  argued
E  worried

Ⓐ  Ⓑ  Ⓒ  Ⓓ  Ⓔ

**46  You can conclude that the boys**
A  are having fun   B  will be caught
C  will both run for it   D  have no problems
E  are busy eating apples

Ⓐ  Ⓑ  Ⓒ  Ⓓ  Ⓔ

**47  'Stealthily' means the same as**
A  quietly and carefully   B  quickly   C  fortunately
D  boldly   E  loudly

Ⓐ  Ⓑ  Ⓒ  Ⓓ  Ⓔ

**48** **Tom probably attracted the attention of the well-dressed man by**
A climbing the tree   B picking the apples
C dropping the apples   D calling out to Joe
E his love of apples

Ⓐ   Ⓑ   Ⓒ   Ⓓ   Ⓔ

**49** **'Luscious' means the same as**
A red   B ripe   C pretty   D plenty   E delicious

Ⓐ   Ⓑ   Ⓒ   Ⓓ   Ⓔ

**50** **To get to the tree the boys had to**
A run fast   B climb a fence
C crawl through a hedge   D climb a wall
E open the gate

Ⓐ   Ⓑ   Ⓒ   Ⓓ   Ⓔ

**51** **The expression 'Joe "froze" ' means**
A he became ice   B he was very cold
C he stood absolutely still   D he ran   E he was wet

Ⓐ   Ⓑ   Ⓒ   Ⓓ   Ⓔ

Choose the word that is opposite in meaning to the one in capitals.

**52** **IMMINENT**
A close   B remote   C scarce   D neat   E clean

Ⓐ   Ⓑ   Ⓒ   Ⓓ   Ⓔ

**53** **PRINCIPAL**
A chief   B belief   C subordinate   D head   E quick

Ⓐ   Ⓑ   Ⓒ   Ⓓ   Ⓔ

**54** **SIMPLE**
A similar   B small   C easy   D complex   E pure

Ⓐ   Ⓑ   Ⓒ   Ⓓ   Ⓔ

**55** **SORROW**
A joy   B grief   C tears   D sadness   E people

Ⓐ   Ⓑ   Ⓒ   Ⓓ   Ⓔ

**56** **EXTERIOR**
A far   B exercise   C inside   D outside   E soon

Ⓐ   Ⓑ   Ⓒ   Ⓓ   Ⓔ

**57** **SOLID**
A sure   B good   C heavy   D liquid   E hard

Ⓐ   Ⓑ   Ⓒ   Ⓓ   Ⓔ

**58** **FAME**
A dishonour   B glory   C renown   D crown   E kind

Ⓐ   Ⓑ   Ⓒ   Ⓓ   Ⓔ

**59  PERMANENT**
A plenty  B always  C favourable  D temporary
E worker

(A) (B) (C) (D) (E)

**60  FURY**
A fast  B calm  C anger  D winds  E fierce

(A) (B) (C) (D) (E)

**61  RECALL**
A forget  B ready  C shout  D remember  E sound

(A) (B) (C) (D) (E)

**62  INNOCENT**
A child  B troublesome  C goodness  D guilty
E happy

(A) (B) (C) (D) (E)

Choose the word which correctly completes each phrase.

**63  went according …… plan**
A as  B for  C into  D about  E to

(A) (B) (C) (D) (E)

**64  is an authority …… horses**
A at  B beside  C upon  D on  E with

(A) (B) (C) (D) (E)

**65  sailed …… the river**
A around  B across  C through  D in  E before

(A) (B) (C) (D) (E)

**66  shared the apple …… two boys**
A between  B for  C among  D over  E from

(A) (B) (C) (D) (E)

**67  fell ……. the table**
A at  B under  C down  D into  E after

(A) (B) (C) (D) (E)

**68  ran ……. the track**
A before  B under  C around  D about  E through

(A) (B) (C) (D) (E)

**69  flew his kite …… the treetops**
A around  B into  C off  D down  E before

(A) (B) (C) (D) (E)

**70  turned …… the water**
A off  B for  C down  D against  E around

(A) (B) (C) (D) (E)

In each of the following sentences choose the word which
completes the sentence correctly.

**71  The heavy rains made the roads …… so that all vehicles
were unable to use them.**
A impossible  B inestimable  C improbable
D impassable  E safe

(A) (B) (C) (D) (E)

**72** After the long and tiring journey it was a ……. to get home.

A relief  B releave  C happiness  D great  E well

Ⓐ Ⓑ Ⓒ Ⓓ Ⓔ

**73** I did not want to see the movie again as I had seen it on a …… occasion.

A first  B previous  C prime  D precious  E early

Ⓐ Ⓑ Ⓒ Ⓓ Ⓔ

**74** Tom believes his performance is ……. to mine but I know better.

A superior  B better  C good  D successful
E superb

Ⓐ Ⓑ Ⓒ Ⓓ Ⓔ

**75** I was ……. when the magician pulled a rabbit from his hat.

A frightened  B sure  C quick  D astonished
E safe

Ⓐ Ⓑ Ⓒ Ⓓ Ⓔ

**76** His ……. driving caused a serious accident.

A careful  B carefree  C careless  D quick
E clever

Ⓐ Ⓑ Ⓒ Ⓓ Ⓔ

**77** The man was …… to die for his crime.

A condemned  B confused  C confessed
D innocent  E convicted

Ⓐ Ⓑ Ⓒ Ⓓ Ⓔ

**78** The company was ……. sixty years ago.

A built  B established  C made  D due  E upset

Ⓐ Ⓑ Ⓒ Ⓓ Ⓔ

**79** Sugar …… in water to which lime juice has been added makes a refreshing drink.

A sweetened  B put  C dissolved  D stirred
E lumps

Ⓐ Ⓑ Ⓒ Ⓓ Ⓔ

In each of the following find which word is wrongly used.

**80**
    **A**       **B**  **C**  **D**    **E**
Jan's body wait is the same as mine.

Ⓐ Ⓑ Ⓒ Ⓓ Ⓔ

**81**
       **A**               **B**         **C**
When the Prime Minister entered the room everyone

    **D**     **E**
raised from his seat.

Ⓐ Ⓑ Ⓒ Ⓓ Ⓔ

             **A B        C   D     E**
82  I am not sure who is the tallest of the two girls.        Ⓐ  Ⓑ  Ⓒ  Ⓓ  Ⓔ

         **A        B       C    D                E**
83  The man and his wife was waiting to see the principal.    Ⓐ  Ⓑ  Ⓒ  Ⓓ  Ⓔ

    **A        B     C      D     E**
84  All the students but Mary is in uniform today.           Ⓐ  Ⓑ  Ⓒ  Ⓓ  Ⓔ

        **A        B        C         D**
85  Neither Tom nor Mary were there when the accident        Ⓐ  Ⓑ  Ⓒ  Ⓓ  Ⓔ

        **E**
    happened.

             **A   B      C            D      E**
86  The building was constructed from concrete and steal.    Ⓐ  Ⓑ  Ⓒ  Ⓓ  Ⓔ

        **A      B C        D        E**
87  Everyone who is supposed to come are here now.           Ⓐ  Ⓑ  Ⓒ  Ⓓ  Ⓔ

        **A      B          C    D   E**
88  Nobody know the answer to the question.                  Ⓐ  Ⓑ  Ⓒ  Ⓓ  Ⓔ

             **A       B       C        D    E**
89  They were all glad to know she were coming to the picnic. Ⓐ  Ⓑ  Ⓒ  Ⓓ  Ⓔ


In each of the following sentences choose the sentence that is
correctly punctuated.

90  **A** The farmer grew corn, peas, tomatoes, carrots and     Ⓐ  Ⓑ  Ⓒ  Ⓓ  Ⓔ
        cabbages on his farm.
    **B** The farmer grew corn peas, tomatoes, carrots and
        cabbages on his farm.
    **C** The farmer, grew corn, peas tomatoes, carrots and
        cabbages on his farm.
    **D** The farmer grew corn, peas, tomatoes, carrots, and
        cabbages on his farm.
    **E** The farmer grew corn peas tomatoes carrots and
        cabbages on his farm.

91  **A** 'Welcome back,' said the teacher, we are glad you are  Ⓐ  Ⓑ  Ⓒ  Ⓓ  Ⓔ
        well again.

**B** 'Welcome back, said the teacher, we are glad you are well again.'

**C** 'Welcome back,' said the teacher, 'we are glad you are well again.'

**D** 'Welcome back said the teacher 'we are glad you are well again.'

**E** 'Welcome back, said the teacher', 'we are glad you are well again'.

**92**
**A** We will if nothing happens to delay us start our journey at dawn.

**B** We will, if nothing happens to delay us, start our journey at dawn.

**C** We will if nothing happens to delay us, start our journey, at dawn.

**D** We will, if nothing happens, to delay us, start our journey, at dawn.

**E** We will, if nothing happens to delay us start our journey at dawn.

Ⓐ Ⓑ Ⓒ Ⓓ Ⓔ

**93**
**A** Halt, commanded a stern voice.

**B** 'Halt', commanded a stern voice

**C** 'Halt!' commanded a stern voice.

**D** 'Halt, commanded a stern voice'

**E** 'Halt, commanded a stern voice!'

Ⓐ Ⓑ Ⓒ Ⓓ Ⓔ

**94**
**A** The children searched in vain the lost dog could not be found.

**B** The children searched, in vain, the lost dog could not be found

**C** The children searched in vain. The lost dog could not be found.

**D** The children searched in vain: the lost dog could not be found.

**E** The children, searched in vain, the lost dog could not be found.

Ⓐ Ⓑ Ⓒ Ⓓ Ⓔ

**95**
**A** Where did you lose your watch? asked Mother.

**B** Where, did you, lose your watch? asked Mother.

**C** 'Where did you lose your watch?' asked Mother.

**D** 'Where did your lose your watch? asked Mother.'

**E** Where did you lose your watch asked Mother.

Ⓐ Ⓑ Ⓒ Ⓓ Ⓔ

In each of the following choose the word that means the same as the word in capitals.

**96  FICTION**
   **A** not true   **B** story   **C** true   **D** read   **E** book

   Ⓐ   Ⓑ   Ⓒ   Ⓓ   Ⓔ

**97  PRECISE**
   **A** exact   **B** unclear   **C** punctual   **D** necessary
   **E** wrong

   Ⓐ   Ⓑ   Ⓒ   Ⓓ   Ⓔ

**98  EXHAUSTED**
   **A** hurry   **B** tired   **C** energetic   **D** glad   **E** worry

   Ⓐ   Ⓑ   Ⓒ   Ⓓ   Ⓔ

**99  RESPONSE**
   **A** answer   **B** murmured   **C** played   **D** sang
   **E** dumb

   Ⓐ   Ⓑ   Ⓒ   Ⓓ   Ⓔ

**100  GRATITUDE**
   **A** great   **B** love   **C** thanks   **D** eager   **E** ungrateful

   Ⓐ   Ⓑ   Ⓒ   Ⓓ   Ⓔ

# PAPER FIVE

Read the following passage carefully then shade in the oval which gives the correct answer.

There is a magic to an island, that seems to elude larger countries. Perhaps it's the coconut trees waving in the breeze or the sparkling blue waters which beckon so invitingly. Or is it the voices of its people raised in song as they work, or the music which seems to throb in the air? Whatever it is, there is something that makes an island special, something that defies description, but which is so strongly felt. For here nature reveals itself in all its glory.

1   **The magical quality referred to in the passage is**
    **A** found only in large countries
    **B** not found in any country
    **C** found in Africa
    **D** found only in Barbados
    **E** found in islands

Ⓐ  Ⓑ  Ⓒ  Ⓓ  Ⓔ

2   **The blue waters refer to**
    **A** the ocean   **B** a river   **C** a pond   **D** a lake
    **E** a stream

Ⓐ  Ⓑ  Ⓒ  Ⓓ  Ⓔ

3   **'Beckon' means the same as**
    **A** shout   **B** call   **C** sail   **D** swim   **E** sun-bathe

Ⓐ  Ⓑ  Ⓒ  Ⓓ  Ⓔ

4   **Island people appear to be**
    **A** happy   **B** sad   **C** cross   **D** lonely   **E** unfriendly

Ⓐ  Ⓑ  Ⓒ  Ⓓ  Ⓔ

5   **'Defies description' means the same as**
    **A** is difficult to explain   **B** is annoying   **C** is good
    **D** is beautiful   **E** is enjoyable

Ⓐ  Ⓑ  Ⓒ  Ⓓ  Ⓔ

6   **The thing which makes an island special is**
    **A** its people   **B** the scenery
    **C** something difficult to define   **D** its music
    **E** the coconut trees

Ⓐ  Ⓑ  Ⓒ  Ⓓ  Ⓔ

44

In each of the following sentences shade in the oval which has the correct spelling for the word underlined.

7  John <u>dose</u> not understand English, he speaks Spanish.
   **A** doos  **B** does  **C** doze  **D** doez  **E** duz

Ⓐ  Ⓑ  Ⓒ  Ⓓ  Ⓔ

8  The bus had to change its usual <u>root</u> as the road was being repaired.
   **A** roote  **B** rout  **C** route  **D** rute  **E** ruote

Ⓐ  Ⓑ  Ⓒ  Ⓓ  Ⓔ

9  Mr Brown is a <u>tobbacco</u> farmer.
   **A** tobaco  **B** tubbaco  **C** tobbaco  **D** tobacco
   **E** tobacko

Ⓐ  Ⓑ  Ⓒ  Ⓓ  Ⓔ

10  She lost her <u>valueable</u> diamond ring.
    **A** valuble  **B** vallueable  **C** valuable  **D** valluable
    **E** valeuably

Ⓐ  Ⓑ  Ⓒ  Ⓓ  Ⓔ

11  I like this place. It is quiet and <u>peaseful</u>.
    **A** peeceful  **B** peaceful  **C** peceful  **D** peseful
    **E** pieceful

Ⓐ  Ⓑ  Ⓒ  Ⓓ  Ⓔ

12  To the <u>amuzement</u> of everyone the clown's hat fell off.
    **A** amusement  **B** amuezement  **C** amusment
    **D** amoozement  **E** amuzment

Ⓐ  Ⓑ  Ⓒ  Ⓓ  Ⓔ

13  I <u>appreshate</u> your kindness.
    **A** apreshait  **B** appreshiate  **C** aprecate
    **D** appreciate  **E** appriceate

Ⓐ  Ⓑ  Ⓒ  Ⓓ  Ⓔ

14  The congregation rose to sing a <u>hym</u>.
    **A** him  **B** hymn  **C** hyme  **D** heem  **E** hynm

Ⓐ  Ⓑ  Ⓒ  Ⓓ  Ⓔ

15  Please don't <u>menshion</u> what I said to anyone.
    **A** mension  **B** menton  **C** menshon  **D** menson
    **E** mention

Ⓐ  Ⓑ  Ⓒ  Ⓓ  Ⓔ

16  The <u>celler</u> of the house was filled with all sorts of discarded articles.
    **A** seller  **B** sellar  **C** cellar  **D** cellur  **E** sellor

Ⓐ  Ⓑ  Ⓒ  Ⓓ  Ⓔ

In each of the following sentences choose the word that means the same as the word underlined.

**17** **Mother told Jane to buy some stationery at the pharmacy so that she could get started on her correspondence.**
**A** pens   **B** cough medicine   **C** bread and butter
**D** writing paper and envelopes   **E** smelling salts

Ⓐ Ⓑ Ⓒ Ⓓ Ⓔ

**18** **His name was omitted from the list of players by error.**
**A** added   **B** written   **C** numbered   **D** included
**E** dropped

Ⓐ Ⓑ Ⓒ Ⓓ Ⓔ

**19** **The visitors are scheduled to arrive at noon but were very late.**
**A** supposed   **B** asked   **C** determined   **D** timed
**E** going

Ⓐ Ⓑ Ⓒ Ⓓ Ⓔ

**20** **The room where the party was to be held was spacious and beautifully decorated.**
**A** small   **B** old   **C** confined   **D** clean   **E** large

Ⓐ Ⓑ Ⓒ Ⓓ Ⓔ

**21** **Not many people can endure severe pain without fainting.**
**A** bear   **B** feel   **C** have   **D** cure   **E** want

Ⓐ Ⓑ Ⓒ Ⓓ Ⓔ

**22** **The doors were made of solid wood so the burglars were unable to break in.**
**A** heavy   **B** soft   **C** good   **D** brown   **E** old

Ⓐ Ⓑ Ⓒ Ⓓ Ⓔ

**23** **The principal's fury at the boys' behaviour resulted in a severe punishment.**
**A** joy   **B** gratitude   **C** laughter   **D** anger   **E** pride

Ⓐ Ⓑ Ⓒ Ⓓ Ⓔ

**24** **This is a modern building, it was completed only last year.**
**A** large   **B** old   **C** beautiful   **D** useful   **E** new

Ⓐ Ⓑ Ⓒ Ⓓ Ⓔ

**25** **The boy's loyalty to his friends caused him to be punished for something he had not done.**
**A** goodness   **B** happiness   **C** cruelty
**D** faithfulness   **E** unkindness

Ⓐ Ⓑ Ⓒ Ⓓ Ⓔ

**26** **Descending from the mountains was much easier than climbing up.**
**A** viewing   **B** the beauty   **C** going down   **D** falling
**E** describing

Ⓐ Ⓑ Ⓒ Ⓓ Ⓔ

**27** John is an <u>obedient</u> boy, he always follows his mother's instructions.

A dutiful   B helpful   C bad   D kind   E lazy

(A)   (B)   (C)   (D)   (E)

In each of the following sentences a word is incorrectly used. Find out which one.

     A   B    C     D     E
**28** I have never know a more faithful worker than Joe.

(A)   (B)   (C)   (D)   (E)

     A     B   C   D       E
**29** Nobody have any idea of what happened to the toys.

(A)   (B)   (C)   (D)   (E)

        A    B   C D E
**30** The new house is for sail.

(A)   (B)   (C)   (D)   (E)

        A   B     C    D       E
**31** The sun shine brightly in the morning.

(A)   (B)   (C)   (D)   (E)

        A      B   C   D   E
**32** The girl and her friend was here today.

(A)   (B)   (C)   (D)   (E)

     A   B      C     D       E
**33** Each of the chairs have a number on it.

(A)   (B)   (C)   (D)   (E)

        A      B     C   D   E
**34** The polite gentleman rose his hat to the lady.

(A)   (B)   (C)   (D)   (E)

     A       B C D      E
**35** Neither the boy or his father came to meet the teacher.

(A)   (B)   (C)   (D)   (E)

     A      B      C   D   E
**36** All the apples on the tree was ripe.

(A)   (B)   (C)   (D)   (E)

     A B   C   D   E
**37** I forget to take my homework to school this morning.

(A)   (B)   (C)   (D)   (E)

In each of the following select the form of the words in capitals which best completes the sentence.

**38** **DRAW**   The carriage was ...... by four white horses.

A draws   B drawn   C drew   D drove   E drewed

(A)   (B)   (C)   (D)   (E)

**39  INVENT**   His father is a famous ......
**A** invents   **B** invention   **C** inventing   **D** invented
**E** inventor

    Ⓐ   Ⓑ   Ⓒ   Ⓓ   Ⓔ

**40  ARRIVE**   He ...... in time for the movie though we thought he would have been late.
**A** arrived   **B** arrival   **C** arrives   **D** arriving   **E** come

    Ⓐ   Ⓑ   Ⓒ   Ⓓ   Ⓔ

**41  EXPLAIN**   His ...... of his late arrival was not accepted by his employer.
**A** explained   **B** explains   **C** explaining
**D** explanation   **E** apology

    Ⓐ   Ⓑ   Ⓒ   Ⓓ   Ⓔ

**42  BUILD**   This is the house that Mr Jones has just ......
**A** builds   **B** built   **C** builded   **D** building
**E** bought

    Ⓐ   Ⓑ   Ⓒ   Ⓓ   Ⓔ

**43  SPEAK**   She ...... both Spanish and English fluently so the other students often ask for her help.
**A** spoke   **B** spoken   **C** speaking   **D** speaks   **E** talk

    Ⓐ   Ⓑ   Ⓒ   Ⓓ   Ⓔ

**44  PROSPER**   Mr Barnes has a ...... business but he had to work hard to make this possible.
**A** prosperous   **B** prospers   **C** prospering
**D** prospered   **E** prospect

    Ⓐ   Ⓑ   Ⓒ   Ⓓ   Ⓔ

**45  COMFORT**   She sat in the most ...... chair in the room.
**A** comforting   **B** comforts   **C** comforted
**D** comfortful   **E** comfortable

    Ⓐ   Ⓑ   Ⓒ   Ⓓ   Ⓔ

**46  LIFE**   My dressmaker ...... on Main Street.
**A** living   **B** lives   **C** live   **D** liveth   **E** stays

    Ⓐ   Ⓑ   Ⓒ   Ⓓ   Ⓔ

**47  BELIEVE**   It is my ...... that she is telling the truth.
**A** believing   **B** believes   **C** believed   **D** idea
**E** belief

    Ⓐ   Ⓑ   Ⓒ   Ⓓ   Ⓔ

Read the following passage carefully then choose the correct answer.

Oh to be young and free! The happiest and most beautiful sounds are those of laughing children noisily at play. How they sing and dance and caper without a care, their radiant faces alight with pleasure in the simple childish things which make childhood so dear.

**48** **Children at play are**
  **A** noisy  **B** scared  **C** sad  **D** fighting  **E** difficult

Ⓐ  Ⓑ  Ⓒ  Ⓓ  Ⓔ

**49** **Children are able to enjoy**
  **A** sunshine,  **B** happiness  **C** fame
  **D** simple pleasures  **E** good food

Ⓐ  Ⓑ  Ⓒ  Ⓓ  Ⓔ

**50** **Radiant means the same as**
  **A** dark  **B** pretty  **C** red  **D** round  **E** beaming

Ⓐ  Ⓑ  Ⓒ  Ⓓ  Ⓔ

**51** **Youth should be a time of**
  **A** growing  **B** working  **C** freedom and happiness
  **D** beauty  **E** love

Ⓐ  Ⓑ  Ⓒ  Ⓓ  Ⓔ

**52** **You can tell that the writer**
  **A** is annoyed by noise  **B** is sad  **C** is old
  **D** doesn't care for children
  **E** enjoys seeing happy children

Ⓐ  Ⓑ  Ⓒ  Ⓓ  Ⓔ

**53** **Caper means the same as**
  **A** leap  **B** climb  **C** shout  **D** smile  **E** sing

Ⓐ  Ⓑ  Ⓒ  Ⓓ  Ⓔ

**54** **Without a care means**
  **A** careless  **B** cruel  **C** carefree  **D** careful
  **E** cautious

Ⓐ  Ⓑ  Ⓒ  Ⓓ  Ⓔ

In each of the following sentences choose the word which means the same as the word underlined.

**55** **The prisoner broke out of jail and the police are now searching for him.**
  **A** jumped  **B** escaped  **C** fought  **D** got away
  **E** was ill

Ⓐ  Ⓑ  Ⓒ  Ⓓ  Ⓔ

**56** **The principal asked the boys to report to her office at once.**
  **A** now  **B** immediately  **C** quickly  **D** soon
  **E** in a hurry

Ⓐ  Ⓑ  Ⓒ  Ⓓ  Ⓔ

**57** **The boys made up their minds to go camping even though the weather looked gloomy.**
  **A** decided  **B** said  **C** planned  **D** packed
  **E** started

Ⓐ  Ⓑ  Ⓒ  Ⓓ  Ⓔ

**58** John is always <u>at school on time</u>.
A good  B punctual  C late  D early  E everyday

〔Ⓐ Ⓑ Ⓒ Ⓓ Ⓔ〕

**59** He made a <u>hundred runs</u> in the cricket match.
A decade  B century  C score  D dozen  E million

〔Ⓐ Ⓑ Ⓒ Ⓓ Ⓔ〕

**60** The carnival celebrations are held <u>once a year</u>.
A bi-annually  B annually  C fortnightly
C semi-annually  E termly

〔Ⓐ Ⓑ Ⓒ Ⓓ Ⓔ〕

**61** When the man was found to be innocent he was <u>allowed to go</u>.
A released  B punished  C lectured
D imprisoned  E bailed

〔Ⓐ Ⓑ Ⓒ Ⓓ Ⓔ〕

**62** The couple decided to have a party at <u>just after sunset</u>.
A happy  B noon  C dawn  D dark  E twilight

〔Ⓐ Ⓑ Ⓒ Ⓓ Ⓔ〕

**63** Jane <u>said she was sorry</u> for being rude to the teacher.
A appreciated  B told  C apologised  D shouted
E pouted

〔Ⓐ Ⓑ Ⓒ Ⓓ Ⓔ〕

In each of the following choose the word similar in meaning to the words in capitals.

**64** AMPLE
A plentiful  B scare  C foot  D small  E easy

〔Ⓐ Ⓑ Ⓒ Ⓓ Ⓔ〕

**65** FAME
A careless  B rich  C singer  D renown
E happiness

〔Ⓐ Ⓑ Ⓒ Ⓓ Ⓔ〕

**66** CONTRACT
A agreement  B catch  C enlarge  D pause  E plea

〔Ⓐ Ⓑ Ⓒ Ⓓ Ⓔ〕

**67** CUNNING
A queer  B ingenious  C quick  D dull  E artless

〔Ⓐ Ⓑ Ⓒ Ⓓ Ⓔ〕

**68** DISTINCT
A big  B displayed  C clear  D visible  E vague

〔Ⓐ Ⓑ Ⓒ Ⓓ Ⓔ〕

**69** VAIN
A modest  B plain  C cute  D right  E proud

〔Ⓐ Ⓑ Ⓒ Ⓓ Ⓔ〕

**70** ASTONISH
A surprise  B joy  C grief  D abundant  E cheered

〔Ⓐ Ⓑ Ⓒ Ⓓ Ⓔ〕

**71 VISIBLE**
A clear   B seen   C hard   D edible   E new

Ⓐ   Ⓑ   Ⓒ   Ⓓ   Ⓔ

**72 FUNCTIONS**
A neglect   B presentation   C works   D fun
E joins

Ⓐ   Ⓑ   Ⓒ   Ⓓ   Ⓔ

In each of the following choose the word which correctly completes the phrase.

**73   drove ...... the busy street**
A around   B upon   C down   D before   E for

Ⓐ   Ⓑ   Ⓒ   Ⓓ   Ⓔ

**74   placed the book ...... the desk**
A at   B before   C over   D on   E above

Ⓐ   Ⓑ   Ⓒ   Ⓓ   Ⓔ

**75   kept the sugar ...... a jar**
A on   B in   C at   D under   E beside

Ⓐ   Ⓑ   Ⓒ   Ⓓ   Ⓔ

**76   placed the ladder ...... the wall**
A against   B up   C into   D below   E between

Ⓐ   Ⓑ   Ⓒ   Ⓓ   Ⓔ

**77   ran swiftly ...... the hill**
A off   B above   C through   D down   E underneath

Ⓐ   Ⓑ   Ⓒ   Ⓓ   Ⓔ

**78   did not agree ...... him**
A to   B with   C on   D upon   E without

Ⓐ   Ⓑ   Ⓒ   Ⓓ   Ⓔ

**79   accompanied my friend ...... the movie**
A on   B into   C to   D for   E towards

Ⓐ   Ⓑ   Ⓒ   Ⓓ   Ⓔ

In each of the following choose the word which correctly completes the sentence.

**80   You are attempting what appears to be an ...... task as you will not have the assistance you expect.**
A impossible   B impassable   C correct   D happy
E good

Ⓐ   Ⓑ   Ⓒ   Ⓓ   Ⓔ

**81   The Labour Day ...... moved slowly down the street.**
A period   B proud   C parade   D display
E present

Ⓐ   Ⓑ   Ⓒ   Ⓓ   Ⓔ

**82** He has ...... interests all over town; he is the owner of many shops.

A beautiful  B severe  C kind  D business  E some

Ⓐ Ⓑ Ⓒ Ⓓ Ⓔ

**83** It might be to your ...... to enrol in the course as you'll be better qualified for a job.

A advice  B advantage  C adverse  D better
E good

Ⓐ Ⓑ Ⓒ Ⓓ Ⓔ

**84** The boys were warned not to ...... with the fire extinguishers as this could be dangerous in the event of a fire.

A taper  B disturb  C tamper  D explode  E use

Ⓐ Ⓑ Ⓒ Ⓓ Ⓔ

**85** Don't be discouraged by ...... ; keep trying and you'll succeed.

A falling  B illness  C studying  D failure
E fantasy

Ⓐ Ⓑ Ⓒ Ⓓ Ⓔ

**86** His ...... for the running of the shows seems well thought out and workable.

A proposal  B profit  C perishing  D play
E practice

Ⓐ Ⓑ Ⓒ Ⓓ Ⓔ

**87** Some substances are ...... in water.

A solve  B serious  C soluble  D clean  E great

Ⓐ Ⓑ Ⓒ Ⓓ Ⓔ

**88** The ...... of the forest made our camping trip unpleasant.

A health  B freshness  C air  D humidity
E horizon

Ⓐ Ⓑ Ⓒ Ⓓ Ⓔ

In each of the following choose the sentence with the best expression.

**89** A John and Tom are good friends; they constantly together.
  B John and Tom are good friends; they are constantly together.
  C John and Tom is good friends; they are constantly together.
  D John and Tom was good friends; they are constantly together.
  E John and Tom be good friends; they are constantly together.

Ⓐ Ⓑ Ⓒ Ⓓ Ⓔ

**90**
A The teacher said the girl impolite.
B The teacher call the girl impolite.
C The teacher told the girl she was impolite.
D The teacher tell the girl she was impolite.
E The teacher say the girl was impolite.

   Ⓐ  Ⓑ  Ⓒ  Ⓓ  Ⓔ

**91**
A Holding onto moving vehicle is dangerous.
B It is dangerous to hold on to a moving vehicle.
C When vehicles moving you shouldn't hold onto it.
D To hold onto a moving vehicle is dangerous.
E If you hold onto a moving vehicle it can be dangerous.

   Ⓐ  Ⓑ  Ⓒ  Ⓓ  Ⓔ

**92**
A Christmas usually everyone have a happy time.
B Christmas is usually a happy time for everyone.
C Everyone is usually happy at Christmas time.
D When Christmas come everyone is happy.
E Christmas time bring happiness for everyone.

   Ⓐ  Ⓑ  Ⓒ  Ⓓ  Ⓔ

**93**
A The bumpy roads made the long drive most uncomfortable.
B The uncomfortable ride was because of the bumpy road.
C When the road bumpy the ride really uncomfortable.
D Uncomfortable rides are always on bumpy roads.
E The bumpy roads makes the long drive uncomfortable.

   Ⓐ  Ⓑ  Ⓒ  Ⓓ  Ⓔ

In each of the following choose the word that is opposite in meaning to the word in capitals.

**94 ADVANCE**
A forward  B retreat  C give  D lend  E borrow

   Ⓐ  Ⓑ  Ⓒ  Ⓓ  Ⓔ

**95 EXPAND**
A big  B clean  C plain  D contract  E bulge

   Ⓐ  Ⓑ  Ⓒ  Ⓓ  Ⓔ

**96 CEASE**
A start  B help  C front  D end  E find

   Ⓐ  Ⓑ  Ⓒ  Ⓓ  Ⓔ

**97 EXIT**
A theatre  B door  C out  D go  E entrance

   Ⓐ  Ⓑ  Ⓒ  Ⓓ  Ⓔ

## 98 WILD
A wolf   B tame   C animal   D bad   E dangerous

    Ⓐ   Ⓑ   Ⓒ   Ⓓ   Ⓔ

## 99 FREQUENT
A often   B far   C for nothing   D seldom   E soft

    Ⓐ   Ⓑ   Ⓒ   Ⓓ   Ⓔ

## 100 LIBERTY
A freedom   B sadness   C slavery   D generous
E powerful

    Ⓐ   Ⓑ   Ⓒ   Ⓓ   Ⓔ

# PAPER SIX

In each of the following select the word that could be used instead of the phrase underlined.

1  Mr Brown sent Kurt to collect the plates from the <u>dog's shelter</u>.
   A kennel   B basement   C lounge   D kitchen
   E backyard

(A)  (B)  (C)  (D)  (E)

2  The milkman took the milk to the <u>place where butter is made</u>.
   A diary   B factory   C shop   D dairy   E industry

(A)  (B)  (C)  (D)  (E)

3  The government was <u>selected by a few people</u>.
   A a democracy   B a bureaucracy   C an oligarchy
   D an aristocracy   E a plutocracy

(A)  (B)  (C)  (D)  (E)

4  The management complained of <u>acts of wilful damage</u> by the workers.
   A rioting   B disturbances   C sabotage   D strikes
   E support

(A)  (B)  (C)  (D)  (E)

5  The teacher told the student to study the <u>matter which settled at the bottom of the test tube</u>.
   A matter   B sediment   C material   D remnant
   E remains

(A)  (B)  (C)  (D)  (E)

6  The art students assembled a <u>picture of small pieces of coloured glass</u>.
   A mosaic   B skeleton   C batik   D profile
   E caricature

(A)  (B)  (C)  (D)  (E)

7  The pirates hid the goods on the <u>flat bottomed boat</u>.
   A ship   B canoe   C submarine   D barge   E ferry

(A)  (B)  (C)  (D)  (E)

8  'Look at the <u>list for your duties</u>,' said the teacher.
   A roster   B blackboard   C queue   D bulletin
   E menu

(A)  (B)  (C)  (D)  (E)

In each of the following choose the word which correctly completes each sentence.

9  You should go ...... now. It is getting late.
   A after   B behind   C from   D into   E in

(A)  (B)  (C)  (D)  (E)

10  He left me ...... a word.
    **A** between  **B** with  **C** without  **D** at  **E** in

    Ⓐ  Ⓑ  Ⓒ  Ⓓ  Ⓔ

11  The families had come far ...... their homes.
    **A** into  **B** from  **C** behind  **D** without  **E** on

    Ⓐ  Ⓑ  Ⓒ  Ⓓ  Ⓔ

12  She fell ...... the tree.
    **A** at  **B** in  **C** from  **D** away  **E** between

    Ⓐ  Ⓑ  Ⓒ  Ⓓ  Ⓔ

13  It was ...... his dignity to accept the defeat.
    **A** along  **B** with  **C** in  **D** between  **E** beneath

    Ⓐ  Ⓑ  Ⓒ  Ⓓ  Ⓔ

14  She ordered him ...... the premises.
    **A** by  **B** on  **C** behind  **D** around  **E** off

    Ⓐ  Ⓑ  Ⓒ  Ⓓ  Ⓔ

15  The boat sailed ...... the bridge.
    **A** behind  **B** around  **C** under  **D** up  **E** off

    Ⓐ  Ⓑ  Ⓒ  Ⓓ  Ⓔ

16  He was left ...... a cent.
    **A** onto  **B** from  **C** off  **D** nearby  **E** without

    Ⓐ  Ⓑ  Ⓒ  Ⓓ  Ⓔ

Read the following sentences carefully and then choose the
word which correctly names the parts of speech of the
underlined words.

17  **Captain Scott was a <u>famous</u> explorer.**
    **A** noun  **B** adverb  **C** pronoun  **D** conjunction
    **E** adjective

    Ⓐ  Ⓑ  Ⓒ  Ⓓ  Ⓔ

18  **Mrs James was absent <u>yesterday</u>.**
    **A** pronoun  **B** adverb  **C** preposition  **D** noun
    **E** adjective

    Ⓐ  Ⓑ  Ⓒ  Ⓓ  Ⓔ

19  **The boy handed his teacher a <u>bouquet</u> of flowers.**
    **A** preposition  **B** conjunction  **C** noun  **D** pronoun
    **E** adjective

    Ⓐ  Ⓑ  Ⓒ  Ⓓ  Ⓔ

20  **'This is correct,' commented <u>his</u> friend**
    **A** preposition  **B** adjective  **C** adverb  **D** noun
    **E** pronoun

    Ⓐ  Ⓑ  Ⓒ  Ⓓ  Ⓔ

21  **My house is different <u>from</u> yours.**
    **A** noun  **B** pronoun  **C** adverb  **D** adjective
    **E** preposition

    Ⓐ  Ⓑ  Ⓒ  Ⓓ  Ⓔ

**22** **I am not going over <u>there</u>.**
    **A** adverb  **B** preposition  **C** noun  **D** conjunction
    **E** pronoun

Ⓐ  Ⓑ  Ⓒ  Ⓓ  Ⓔ

In each of the following choose the word that is opposite in meaning to the word in capitals.

**23** **HOPEFUL**
    **A** hopeless  **B** futile  **C** generous  **D** kind
    **E** understanding

Ⓐ  Ⓑ  Ⓒ  Ⓓ  Ⓔ

**24** **PERFECT**
    **A** complete  **B** perfection  **C** faultless  **D** finished
    **E** imperfect

Ⓐ  Ⓑ  Ⓒ  Ⓓ  Ⓔ

**25** **ASSISTANCE**
    **A** resistance  **B** instance  **C** hindrance
    **D** remittance  **E** extravagance

Ⓐ  Ⓑ  Ⓒ  Ⓓ  Ⓔ

**26** **CONTRACT**
    **A** expand  **B** subtract  **C** attract  **D** decrease
    **E** protect

Ⓐ  Ⓑ  Ⓒ  Ⓓ  Ⓔ

**27** **RECKLESS**
    **A** stubborn  **B** needless  **C** cautious  **D** careless
    **E** carefree

Ⓐ  Ⓑ  Ⓒ  Ⓓ  Ⓔ

**28** **VOLUNTARY**
    **A** preparatory  **B** satisfactory  **C** necessary
    **D** compulsory  **E** unavoidable

Ⓐ  Ⓑ  Ⓒ  Ⓓ  Ⓔ

**29** **CONCEITED**
    **A** anxious  **B** modest  **C** deceitful  **D** proud
    **E** corrupt

Ⓐ  Ⓑ  Ⓒ  Ⓓ  Ⓔ

**30** **INFERIOR**
    **A** exterior  **B** interior  **C** junior  **D** senior
    **E** superior

Ⓐ  Ⓑ  Ⓒ  Ⓓ  Ⓔ

Read the following passage carefully then find the correct answer to each question.

All the inhabitants waited eagerly as the animals discussed the news — new people were seen arriving at the Big Farm. The feathered animals speculated about the likely change, some happily, others fearfully. (There was always the possibility of dogs, cats and even worse, boys.) Yet, most importantly, the new arrivals would be planters. It had been five years since there was even a kitchen garden and times had been very hard.

**31  What did the animals talk about first?**
A the boys   B the cats   C the dogs
D the new people   E the Big Farm

Ⓐ  Ⓑ  Ⓒ  Ⓓ  Ⓔ

**32  What was important about the new people?**
A they were planters   B they would bring boys
C they were dishonest
D they would live on the farm
E they would be friendly

Ⓐ  Ⓑ  Ⓒ  Ⓓ  Ⓔ

**33  When the animals heard the news, there was**
A excitement   B unhappiness   C a mixed reaction
D optimism   E happiness

Ⓐ  Ⓑ  Ⓒ  Ⓓ  Ⓔ

**34  Another word for 'hard' is**
A soft   B firm   C solid   D heavy   E difficult

Ⓐ  Ⓑ  Ⓒ  Ⓓ  Ⓔ

**35  From the passage one may conclude that 'inhabitants' means**
A people in the neighbourhood   B the animals
C the new arrivals   D cats   E children

Ⓐ  Ⓑ  Ⓒ  Ⓓ  Ⓔ

**36  A word which means nearly the same as 'speculated' is**
A guessed   B retracted   C substantiated
D demanded   E encouraged

Ⓐ  Ⓑ  Ⓒ  Ⓓ  Ⓔ

**37  The clause 'It had been five years since there was even a kitchen garden' suggests**
A food was plentiful   B food was scarce
C food was being harvested
D food was being planted   E food was abandoned

Ⓐ  Ⓑ  Ⓒ  Ⓓ  Ⓔ

In each following find the correct spelling for the word underlined.

**38  It _ocured_ to me that my friend had forgotten her promise.**
A occurred   B okured   C occured   D ocurred
E okurred

Ⓐ  Ⓑ  Ⓒ  Ⓓ  Ⓔ

**39** I lost my <u>queue</u> for the door.
   **A** quay  **B** key  **C** kay  **D** kee  **E** quieu

Ⓐ Ⓑ Ⓒ Ⓓ Ⓔ

**40** They were standing over <u>their</u>.
   **A** thier  **B** there  **C** ther  **D** theer  **E** thare

Ⓐ Ⓑ Ⓒ Ⓓ Ⓔ

**41** It is not <u>rite</u> that you should do this.
   **A** wright  **B** write  **C** wight  **D** right  **E** ryte

Ⓐ Ⓑ Ⓒ Ⓓ Ⓔ

**42** <u>Allright</u>, I will accompany you.
   **A** all right  **B** alrite  **C** alwright  **D** alright  **E** alrite

Ⓐ Ⓑ Ⓒ Ⓓ Ⓔ

**43** The accident was a horrible <u>cite</u>.
   **A** site  **B** sighte  **C** sight  **D** syte  **E** sieght

Ⓐ Ⓑ Ⓒ Ⓓ Ⓔ

**44** The girl was upset because her father was <u>dieing</u>.
   **A** dieng  **B** dyeing  **C** dying  **D** deing  **E** diying

Ⓐ Ⓑ Ⓒ Ⓓ Ⓔ

**45** After they had finished their shopping, the women
   looked for a refreshment <u>parlo</u>.
   **A** pallor  **B** parluour  **C** parlour  **D** pahlou
   **E** parla

Ⓐ Ⓑ Ⓒ Ⓓ Ⓔ

**46** The school band has <u>wanderful</u> players.
   **A** wunederful  **B** onederfull  **C** wonderfull
   **D** wonderful  **E** wanderfull

Ⓐ Ⓑ Ⓒ Ⓓ Ⓔ

**47** The statistics show that there are more <u>wimmen</u> than
   men.
   **A** wimen  **B** wommen  **C** women  **D** wemen
   **E** wiemen

Ⓐ Ⓑ Ⓒ Ⓓ Ⓔ

**48** I received several presents for my <u>birtday</u>.
   **A** birteday  **B** birthday  **C** berthday
   **D** birtdae  **E** birtheday

Ⓐ Ⓑ Ⓒ Ⓓ Ⓔ

**49** The shoes are correctly priced at twenty <u>dolars</u> per pair.
   **A** dolers  **B** dollirs  **C** dollars  **D** dollers
   **E** dolliers

Ⓐ Ⓑ Ⓒ Ⓓ Ⓔ

**50** The bride wore a lovely <u>saten</u> gown.
   **A** sattin  **B** sateen  **C** satten  **D** satin
   **E** satinn

Ⓐ Ⓑ Ⓒ Ⓓ Ⓔ

**51** Only one <u>him</u> was sung in church this morning.
   **A** hyme  **B** heem  **C** hime  **D** hymn  **E** hym

Ⓐ Ⓑ Ⓒ Ⓓ Ⓔ

**52**  I bought my father a packet of <u>handkerchieves</u>.
A hankerchieves   B handkerchieeves
C handkerchiefs   D hankerchiefs
E handkerchieefs

A   B   C   D   E

**53**  The Smiths moved to a new <u>residens</u>.
A residents   B ressidents   C resedence
D residence   E recidents

A   B   C   D   E

**54**  His <u>motorcycicle</u> has a powerful engine.
A motorsycle   B motercycle   C moturcicle
D motorcycle   E motocycle

A   B   C   D   E

Choose the word which will make each of the following
sentences correct.

**55**  He would not ...... my offer.
A except   B receive   C accept   D accede   E attain

A   B   C   D   E

**56**  No crops could be had from the land because it
was ......
A fertile   B productive   C dry   D barren
E fruitful

A   B   C   D   E

**57**  Not a mango was in sight because the tree was ......
A bear   B bare   C full   D loaded   E sparce

A   B   C   D   E

**58**  You ...... to go.
A aught   B ought   C should   D shouldn't   E must

A   B   C   D   E

**59**  The ...... had ten episodes.
A serial   B cereal   C vegetable   D corn   E porridge

A   B   C   D   E

**60**  In her ...... she had written the important events in her
life.
A dairy   B bosom   C diary   D stationery
E statement

A   B   C   D   E

**61**  The man had to press the ...... to avoid an accident.
A break   B pedal   C peddle   D brake   E lever

A   B   C   D   E

**62**  In ancient days soldiers fought with ......
A missiles   B bombs   C swords   D canyon
E radar

A   B   C   D   E

Choose the sentence which you think is correct.

**63**
  **A** The men were sitting by the door.
  **B** The man were sitting by the door.
  **C** The men was sitting by the door.
  **D** The men has been sitting by the door.
  **E** The man have been sitting by the door.

    Ⓐ  Ⓑ  Ⓒ  Ⓓ  Ⓔ

**64**
  **A** James is much brighter than he is.
  **B** James is much brighter than him.
  **C** James is as bright as he.
  **D** James is as brighter than him.
  **E** James is much bright than he.

    Ⓐ  Ⓑ  Ⓒ  Ⓓ  Ⓔ

**65**
  **A** Let you and me goes to the shore.
  **B** Let you and I go to the shore.
  **C** Let you and me go to the shore.
  **D** Let me and you go to the shore.
  **E** Let me and you goes to the shore.

    Ⓐ  Ⓑ  Ⓒ  Ⓓ  Ⓔ

**66**
  **A** Those are them.
  **B** Those are the ones.
  **C** Those are these.
  **D** The ones is they.
  **E** Those is these.

    Ⓐ  Ⓑ  Ⓒ  Ⓓ  Ⓔ

**67**
  **A** Audrey and she ran to the house.
  **B** She and Audrey ran to the house.
  **C** Audrey and she run to the house.
  **D** Audrey and her ran to the house.
  **E** Audrey and she runs to the house.

    Ⓐ  Ⓑ  Ⓒ  Ⓓ  Ⓔ

Read the following passage carefully then choose the correct answer.

My name is Junior Drummond. I was born in Savanna-la-Mar Westmoreland, my father being employed in the gardens of the large mansion of the Great House. My mother died when I was ten years of age, and my father, when I was fourteen. My uncle, Neville Brown, came west from Kingston and adopted me. For several years I lived very happily with my uncle and his wife Hermine, and at Uncle's death, which occurred four years ago, he left me part of his fortune, twenty-seven thousand dollars. I was then twenty years of age and was greatly interested in calypso. On my uncle's death I returned to my native town, Savanna-la-Mar, where I started a business as a mechanic.

**68** **What is the writer's surname?**
**A** Junior   **B** Smith   **C** Drummond   **D** Jones
**E** Wright

Ⓐ Ⓑ Ⓒ Ⓓ Ⓔ

**69** **What was Junior's aunt's surname?**
**A** Drummond   **B** Hermine   **C** Brown   **D** Mary
**E** Hyacinth

Ⓐ Ⓑ Ⓒ Ⓓ Ⓔ

**70** **Where was Junior's father employed before he died?**
**A** in a band   **B** at the Great House   **C** in Kingston
**D** in Manchester   **E** at the sugar factory

Ⓐ Ⓑ Ⓒ Ⓓ Ⓔ

**71** **Calypso is a kind of**
**A** drink   **B** reggae   **C** music   **D** folk music
**E** classical music

Ⓐ Ⓑ Ⓒ Ⓓ Ⓔ

**72** **What was Junior's native town?**
**A** Kingston   **B** Montego Bay   **C** Savanna-la-Mar
**D** St Elizabeth   **E** Clarendon

Ⓐ Ⓑ Ⓒ Ⓓ Ⓔ

**73** **The word in the passage which means nearly the same as 'went back' is**
**A** employed   **B** occurred   **C** adopted   **D** repeated
**E** returned

Ⓐ Ⓑ Ⓒ Ⓓ Ⓔ

**74** **A mechanic is someone who repairs**
**A** houses   **B** vehicles   **C** bridges   **D** roads
**E** cameras

Ⓐ Ⓑ Ⓒ Ⓓ Ⓔ

**75** **At what age was Junior when he wrote the passage?**
**A** ten   **B** fourteen   **C** twenty-four   **D** twenty
**E** twenty-one

Ⓐ Ⓑ Ⓒ Ⓓ Ⓔ

**76** **The opposite of 'started' is**
**A** commenced   **B** increased   **C** decreased
**D** stopped   **E** completed

Ⓐ Ⓑ Ⓒ Ⓓ Ⓔ

In each of the following sentences find the correctly punctuated sentence.

**77** **A** Stop the noise! the teacher shouted.
**B** 'Stop the noise! the teacher shouted.
**C** 'Stop the noise' the teacher shouted.

Ⓐ Ⓑ Ⓒ Ⓓ Ⓔ

**D** 'Stop the noise,' the teacher shouted.
**E** 'Stop the noise!' the teacher shouted.

**78**
**A** She bought apples, bananas and tomatoes
**B** She bought apples, bananas, and tomatoes.
**C** She bought apples, bananas and tomatoes.
**D** She bought apples, bananas, and tomatoes
**E** She bought apples, bananas and tomatoes;

Ⓐ Ⓑ Ⓒ Ⓓ Ⓔ

**79**
**A** Will you come with me asked June.
**B** 'Will you come with me? asked June.'
**C** Will you come with me asked June?
**D** Will you come with me? asked June.
**E** 'Will you come with me?' asked June.

Ⓐ Ⓑ Ⓒ Ⓓ Ⓔ

**80**
**A** John, the teacher was absent yesterday
**B** John, the teacher, was absent yesterday.
**C** John the teacher was absent yesterday.
**D** John the teacher, was absent yesterday.
**E** John the teacher was absent, yesterday.

Ⓐ Ⓑ Ⓒ Ⓓ Ⓔ

**81**
**A** Where are you going asked Hilary?
**B** Where are you going? asked Hilary.
**C** 'Where are you going'? asked Hilary.
**D** 'Where are you going? asked Hilary.'
**E** 'Where are you going?' asked Hilary.

Ⓐ Ⓑ Ⓒ Ⓓ Ⓔ

In each of the following select the form of the word in capitals which correctly completes the sentence.

**82** **CRUEL** The donkey was subjected to much ......
from its owner.
**A** cruelty **B** cruel **C** cruelsome **D** cruelly
**E** cruelness

Ⓐ Ⓑ Ⓒ Ⓓ Ⓔ

**83** **ANGER** The restaurant owner was very ...... with his
cashier.
**A** angered **B** angry **C** angrier **D** anger
**E** angersome

Ⓐ Ⓑ Ⓒ Ⓓ Ⓔ

**84** **NEIGHBOUR** A new family moved into the ......
**A** neighbours **B** neighboured **C** neighbourhood
**D** neighbouring **E** neighbour

Ⓐ Ⓑ Ⓒ Ⓓ Ⓔ

**85  ATTRACT    The film-star looked very ......**
A attraction   B attracts   C attract   D attractive
E attractiveness

Ⓐ   Ⓑ   Ⓒ   Ⓓ   Ⓔ

**86  ADVENTURE    The pioneers were very ...... when they first arrived.**
A adventured   B adventurous   C advent
D adventures   E advented

Ⓐ   Ⓑ   Ⓒ   Ⓓ   Ⓔ

**87  INVENT    The scientist was awarded a prize for his ......**
A invent   B invents   C invention   D inventive
E inventure

Ⓐ   Ⓑ   Ⓒ   Ⓓ   Ⓔ

**88  ATTEND    The nurse was very ...... to the child.**
A attention   B attentive   C attend   D attends
E attentively

Ⓐ   Ⓑ   Ⓒ   Ⓓ   Ⓔ

**89  ASSIST    The police ...... the firemen in keeping away spectators.**
A assists   B assisting   C assisted   D assistance
E assured

Ⓐ   Ⓑ   Ⓒ   Ⓓ   Ⓔ

**90  COURAGE    The boy was very ......**
A encourage   B encouragement   C courageous
D encouraged   E courage

Ⓐ   Ⓑ   Ⓒ   Ⓓ   Ⓔ

In each of the following find the word that is similar in meaning to the word underlined.

**91  In the litter was a puny kitten.**
A weak   B strong   C brave   D timid   E coward

Ⓐ   Ⓑ   Ⓒ   Ⓓ   Ⓔ

**92  The film show began at midnight.**
A commenced   B finished   C completed   D ended
E begun

Ⓐ   Ⓑ   Ⓒ   Ⓓ   Ⓔ

**93  The minimum wage for domestic workers is thirty dollars per week.**
A maximum   B least   C most   D last   E majority

Ⓐ   Ⓑ   Ⓒ   Ⓓ   Ⓔ

**94  He purchased a large number of exercise books.**
A sold   B released   C bought   D distributed
E collected

Ⓐ   Ⓑ   Ⓒ   Ⓓ   Ⓔ

**95** At last the doctor discovered a <u>remedy</u>.
    **A** cure  **B** raiment  **C** rank  **D** dwelling  **E** illness

(A) (B) (C) (D) (E)

**96** The teacher was tall and <u>slender</u>.
    **A** stout  **B** fat  **C** straight  **D** skinny  **E** slim

(A) (B) (C) (D) (E)

In each of the following sentences choose the word that correctly completes the sentences.

**97** The fox saw a beautiful …… of grapes in the water.
    **A** bunch  **B** flock  **C** gang  **D** bale  **E** batch

(A) (B) (C) (D) (E)

**98** A …… of diamonds was in the centre of her engagement ring.
    **A** clutch  **B** clump  **C** galaxy  **D** cluster
    **E** collection

(A) (B) (C) (D) (E)

**99** A …… of ships was moved into the area.
    **A** flight  **B** crate  **C** forest  **D** pack  **E** fleet

(A) (B) (C) (D) (E)

**100** A …… of cattle was seen along the highway.
    **A** flock  **B** gaggle  **C** herd  **D** horde  **E** host

(A) (B) (C) (D) (E)

# PAPER SEVEN

Read the passage carefully then find the answer.

Jamaica is a land of contrasts, not only in its scenic beauty, but in the material wealth of its people. For while some have so much, many children are suffering from malnutrition, do not own a pair of shoes, search the garbage for food, have the pavement for a pillow and the sky for a roof over their heads. These children have never been to school, have no real home life and are crying out for help. Who will answer their cry? The future of our country may depend on this.

1   **The passage suggests that in Jamaica there is**
   **A** only poverty   **B** only wealth
   **C** only children who never go to school
   **D** many people   **E** both poverty and wealth

   Ⓐ   Ⓑ   Ⓒ   Ⓓ   Ⓔ

2   **The writer is most concerned about**
   **A** the beauty of the country
   **B** the wealth of some people   **C** the old people
   **D** the children   **E** everyone

   Ⓐ   Ⓑ   Ⓒ   Ⓓ   Ⓔ

3   **Many disadvantaged children are sleeping**
   **A** at home in their beds   **B** on the sidewalks
   **C** at a friend's house   **D** in apartments
   **E** in town houses

   Ⓐ   Ⓑ   Ⓒ   Ⓓ   Ⓔ

4   **The children in the story need**
   **A** friends   **B** houses   **C** parents   **D** books   **E** help

   Ⓐ   Ⓑ   Ⓒ   Ⓓ   Ⓔ

5   **Malnutrition means**
   **A** starvation   **B** poverty   **C** not eating
   **D** very poor diet   **E** unhappiness

   Ⓐ   Ⓑ   Ⓒ   Ⓓ   Ⓔ

6   **The country's future may depend on**
   **A** helping these children
   **B** which government is in power
   **C** how the people vote   **D** money
   **E** a good opposition

   Ⓐ   Ⓑ   Ⓒ   Ⓓ   Ⓔ

In each of the following choose the word which best completes each sentence.

7   The beggar ...... accepted the gift he received.
    **A** humbly   **B** almost   **C** greatly   **D** heavily
    **E** completely

    Ⓐ  Ⓑ  Ⓒ  Ⓓ  Ⓔ

8   There is ...... of mangoes this year.
    **A** plentiful   **B** many   **C** an abundance   **D** a lot
    **E** scarcity

    Ⓐ  Ⓑ  Ⓒ  Ⓓ  Ⓔ

9   When he fell he ...... broke the antique vase.
    **A** quickly   **B** luckily   **C** calmly   **D** accidentally
    **E** shakily

    Ⓐ  Ⓑ  Ⓒ  Ⓓ  Ⓔ

10  The boy sat down and ...... what the consequences of
    his actions would be.
    **A** worried   **B** think   **C** pondered   **D** dwell   **E** cried

    Ⓐ  Ⓑ  Ⓒ  Ⓓ  Ⓔ

11  The little girl smiled ...... when she received her prize.
    **A** happily   **B** sadly   **C** carefully   **D** up   **E** badly

    Ⓐ  Ⓑ  Ⓒ  Ⓓ  Ⓔ

12  The food was ...... and we all ate it hungrily.
    **A** stale   **B** old   **C** raw   **D** delicious   **E** spoilt

    Ⓐ  Ⓑ  Ⓒ  Ⓓ  Ⓔ

13  I cannot ...... what happened during the accident.
    **A** see   **B** recall   **C** talk   **D** hurry   **E** know

    Ⓐ  Ⓑ  Ⓒ  Ⓓ  Ⓔ

14  The thief ...... approached the house when it was dark.
    **A** noisily   **B** hurriedly   **C** stealthily   **D** suddenly
    **E** boldly

    Ⓐ  Ⓑ  Ⓒ  Ⓓ  Ⓔ

15  The driver did not ...... that he was turning and so he
    collided with another car.
    **A** accelerate   **B** slow   **C** stop   **D** indicate   **E** hurry

    Ⓐ  Ⓑ  Ⓒ  Ⓓ  Ⓔ

16  The ...... treatment of the prisoners caused a rebellion.
    **A** humane   **B** good   **C** pleasant   **D** anxious
    **E** brutal

    Ⓐ  Ⓑ  Ⓒ  Ⓓ  Ⓔ

In each of the following find the word which means the same or
nearly the same as the word underlined.

17  Parents have an <u>obligation</u> to prepare their children to
    live in an adult world.
    **A** job   **B** chance   **C** duty   **D** happiness   **E** time

    Ⓐ  Ⓑ  Ⓒ  Ⓓ  Ⓔ

18  The sailors had to <u>abandon</u> their sinking ship.
    **A** bail   **B** swim   **C** rescue   **D** radio   **E** leave

    Ⓐ  Ⓑ  Ⓒ  Ⓓ  Ⓔ

**19** The stamp will not <u>adhere</u> to the paper unless it has paste on it.
**A** stick  **B** dirty  **C** wet  **D** crumple  **E** colour

(A) (B) (C) (D) (E)

**20** Classes will <u>resume</u> after lunch.
**A** make better  **B** be soon  **C** stop  **D** start again
**E** end

(A) (B) (C) (D) (E)

**21** It is <u>illegal</u> to exceed the speed limit.
**A** all right  **B** silly  **C** wise  **D** not allowed by law
**E** allowed by law

(A) (B) (C) (D) (E)

**22** He is a <u>shrewd</u> business man, he invested his money wisely and now he is rich.
**A** clever  **B** poor  **C** careful  **D** rich  **E** dishonest

(A) (B) (C) (D) (E)

**23** This is the <u>residence</u> of Mr Brown.
**A** shop  **B** car  **C** business  **D** problem  **E** home

(A) (B) (C) (D) (E)

**24** The boy's poor behaviour made the teacher <u>furious</u>.
**A** happy  **B** angry  **C** laugh  **D** thankful  **E** pleased

(A) (B) (C) (D) (E)

**25** His <u>frank</u> discussion of the matter prevented anyone from becoming upset.
**A** good  **B** quick  **C** open  **D** clear  **E** ready

(A) (B) (C) (D) (E)

**26** If you will <u>permit</u> me, I'll accompany you.
**A** send  **B** allow  **C** make  **D** take  **E** need

(A) (B) (C) (D) (E)

**27** We had <u>adequate</u> food and water for our trip into the mountains.
**A** sufficient  **B** plenty  **C** much  **D** good  **E** tasty

(A) (B) (C) (D) (E)

**28** As the <u>ascent</u> of the mountain became more difficult, some of the campers fell behind.
**A** height  **B** peak  **C** upward movement
**D** going downward  **E** green

(A) (B) (C) (D) (E)

In each of the following find the correct spelling of the words underlined.

**29** Mr Brown has a thriving <u>buisness</u> in town selling ice-cream.
**A** biznez  **B** business  **C** bizness  **D** biuness
**E** buizness

(A) (B) (C) (D) (E)

**30** The driver did not obey the stop <u>syne</u> and this caused an accident.

   **A** sine  **B** sign  **C** signe  **D** syn  **E** sighne

     Ⓐ  Ⓑ  Ⓒ  Ⓓ  Ⓔ

**31** My <u>neice</u> came to visit me during the holidays.

   **A** neece  **B** nease  **C** neise  **D** niece  **E** neace

     Ⓐ  Ⓑ  Ⓒ  Ⓓ  Ⓔ

**32** The bad <u>whether</u> conditions made us postpone our trip.

   **A** weather  **B** wether  **C** wheather  **D** weether
   **E** wethir

     Ⓐ  Ⓑ  Ⓒ  Ⓓ  Ⓔ

**33** Our <u>releif</u> was great when he turned up unharmed.

   **A** releaf  **B** releef  **C** relief  **D** releafe  **E** reelief

     Ⓐ  Ⓑ  Ⓒ  Ⓓ  Ⓔ

**34** When the ball was <u>throne</u>, it went through a window.

   **A** `throwne  **B** throan  **C** throon  **D** thrown
   **E** troan

     Ⓐ  Ⓑ  Ⓒ  Ⓓ  Ⓔ

**35** This is the <u>cite</u> on which the house will be built.

   **A** site  **B** syte  **C** cyte  **D** sight  **E** sighte

     Ⓐ  Ⓑ  Ⓒ  Ⓓ  Ⓔ

**36** I like buns with lots of <u>currents</u> in them.

   **A** currentes  **B** curants  **C** curents  **D** currants
   **E** curantes

     Ⓐ  Ⓑ  Ⓒ  Ⓓ  Ⓔ

**37** The strong <u>breaze</u> blew down our coconut tree.

   **A** breeze  **B** breze  **C** brease  **D** breese  **E** brieze

     Ⓐ  Ⓑ  Ⓒ  Ⓓ  Ⓔ

**38** The doctor told his <u>patience</u> he would be late as he had an emergency.

   **A** patiense  **B** patients  **C** pasience  **D** paysense
   **E** patense

     Ⓐ  Ⓑ  Ⓒ  Ⓓ  Ⓔ

**39** The <u>dessert</u> is a hot dry place.

   **A** dezert  **B** desert  **C** deezert  **D** desirt  **E** descert

     Ⓐ  Ⓑ  Ⓒ  Ⓓ  Ⓔ

**40** John is <u>dependant</u> on his sister to support him as he is an orphan.

   **A** dependent  **B** dispendant  **C** dipendent
   **D** dypendent  **E** deependent

     Ⓐ  Ⓑ  Ⓒ  Ⓓ  Ⓔ

In each of the following sentences choose the one which is correctly punctuated.

**41**  **A** 'I am not going,' said Tom. 'I want to stay here.'
      **B** 'I am not going said Tom, I want to stay here'

     Ⓐ  Ⓑ  Ⓒ  Ⓓ  Ⓔ

69

C I am not going, said Tom, I want to stay here.
D 'I am not going', said Tom, 'I want to stay here'
E 'I am not going, said Tom, I want to stay here'

42 A It was, Harry, who told me, about it.   Ⓐ Ⓑ Ⓒ Ⓓ Ⓔ
B It was Harry, who told me about it.
C 'It was Harry who told me about it'
D It, was Harry, who told me, about it
E It was Harry who told me about it.

43 A 'Where have you been all day?' asked father angrily.   Ⓐ Ⓑ Ⓒ Ⓓ Ⓔ
B 'Where have you been all day, asked father angrily'.
C 'Where have you been all day'? asked father angrily.
D 'Where have you been all day? asked father angrily.
E Where have you been all day? asked father angrily.

44 A Diane, Mary David, Thomas and Mark went to the   Ⓐ Ⓑ Ⓒ Ⓓ Ⓔ
movies.
B Diane Mary, David Thomas, and Mark went to the
movies.
C Diane, Mary, David, Thomas and Mark went to the
movies.
D Diane Mary David Thomas and Mark went to the
movies.
E Diane, Mary, David, Thomas, and Mark went to the
movies.

45 A 'Oh no,' exclaimed the girl, 'I did not do it'.   Ⓐ Ⓑ Ⓒ Ⓓ Ⓔ
B Oh no! exclaimed the girl, I did not do it!
C 'Oh no!' exclaimed the girl, 'I did not do it.'
D 'Oh no', exclaimed the girl, 'I did not do it!'
E 'Oh no', exclaimed the girl, 'I did not do it'!

46 A George the boy who won the race received a gold   Ⓐ Ⓑ Ⓒ Ⓓ Ⓔ
medal.
B 'George, the boy who won the race received a gold
medal'.
C George, the boy who won the race, received a gold
medal.
D George the boy, who won the race, received a gold
medal.
E George the boy who won the race, received a gold
medal.

Read the following passage carefully then choose the correct answer to each question.

Many children who live in the city do not know from where the beautiful fresh vegetables they enjoy come, or how they are grown. Many of these vegetables come from the very dry areas in the Parish of St Elizabeth. The farmers, with the assistance of family members, have managed to overcome some of the problems of drought and have been able to produce a large amount of the vegetables grown in Jamaica.

To do this, farmers practise 'dry farming'. The ground is prepared for the crops, then a special kind of grass is cut and used for covering the fields. This process is called mulching. The crops are planted after the first good shower of rain. The mulching helps to retain the moisture in the soil. This, together with occasional watering of each seedling by hand, keeps the vegetables growing until the next shower of rain. It is a hard life, but it can be rewarding when there is a good yield and a good price for the crops. But sometimes the farmer may lose his whole crop from prolonged drought or too much rain at certain stages in the development of the vegetables.

47   **Many city children are not familiar with**
    **A** vegetables   **B** food   **C** farmers
    **D** the growing of vegetables   **E** rainfall

    Ⓐ   Ⓑ   Ⓒ   Ⓓ   Ⓔ

48   **Mulching helps to**
    **A** keep the soil wet   **B** make the trees tall
    **C** dry out the soil   **D** keep out the rain
    **E** make life easy

    Ⓐ   Ⓑ   Ⓒ   Ⓓ   Ⓔ

49   **Farmers must**
    **A** be lazy   **B** enjoy themselves   **C** watch the sky
    **D** work hard   **E** pray for rain

    Ⓐ   Ⓑ   Ⓒ   Ⓓ   Ⓔ

50   **If St Elizabeth had more rain it would**
    **A** be green and beautiful
    **B** produce more vegetables   **C** grow fewer crops
    **D** be a better place   **E** grow larger tomatoes

    Ⓐ   Ⓑ   Ⓒ   Ⓓ   Ⓔ

51   **Rewarding means the same as**
    **A** hurrying   **B** getting a prize   **C** compensating
    **D** giving   **E** contributing

    Ⓐ   Ⓑ   Ⓒ   Ⓓ   Ⓔ

52   **According to the passage too much rain**
    **A** is always good   **B** falls often   **C** floods the fields
    **D** never falls   **E** can be bad for crops

    Ⓐ   Ⓑ   Ⓒ   Ⓓ   Ⓔ

**53** **Prolonged means the same as**
**A** for a long time   **B** quickly   **C** for a short while
**D** hot weather   **E** bad

Ⓐ   Ⓑ   Ⓒ   Ⓓ   Ⓔ

**54** **To grow vegetables successfully you need a good balance between**
**A** people   **B** farming families
**C** rain and dry periods   **D** hard work and laziness
**E** mulching

Ⓐ   Ⓑ   Ⓒ   Ⓓ   Ⓔ

**55** **Drought refers to**
**A** long periods without rain   **B** rainy weather
**C** good soil   **D** dust   **E** good crops

Ⓐ   Ⓑ   Ⓒ   Ⓓ   Ⓔ

**56** **Assistance means the same as**
**A** help   **B** kindness   **C** duty   **D** habits   **E** number

Ⓐ   Ⓑ   Ⓒ   Ⓓ   Ⓔ

In each of the following choose the letter above the word which is incorrect in the sentence.

     A    B   C   D  E
**57**   John, as well as his friends were late for school.

Ⓐ   Ⓑ   Ⓒ   Ⓓ   Ⓔ

   A     B    C D  E
**58**   Every orange in the box were ripe.

Ⓐ   Ⓑ   Ⓒ   Ⓓ   Ⓔ

   A    B     C  D  E
**59**   Either Tom or Mary are coming today.

Ⓐ   Ⓑ   Ⓒ   Ⓓ   Ⓔ

    A B   C  D     E
**60**   Paul is the biggest of the twins.

Ⓐ   Ⓑ   Ⓒ   Ⓓ   Ⓔ

    A    B   C   D   E
**61**   Nobody are absent from school today.

Ⓐ   Ⓑ   Ⓒ   Ⓓ   Ⓔ

     A    B   C   D      E
**62**   The clown road a white horse in the show.

Ⓐ   Ⓑ   Ⓒ   Ⓓ   Ⓔ

   A   B   C  D    E
**63**   Each boy were given a drink at lunch.

Ⓐ   Ⓑ   Ⓒ   Ⓓ   Ⓔ

     A    B C D E
**64**   My father's car is for sail.

Ⓐ   Ⓑ   Ⓒ   Ⓓ   Ⓔ

    A    B   C   D     E
**65**   No one know who broke the window.

Ⓐ   Ⓑ   Ⓒ   Ⓓ   Ⓔ

```
     A   B   C   D   E
6  None of the children were sick.                    Ⓐ   Ⓑ   Ⓒ   Ⓓ   Ⓔ

         A   B   C       D   E
7  The pretty girl has long black hare.               Ⓐ   Ⓑ   Ⓒ   Ⓓ   Ⓔ

   A   B   C   D   E
8  She has went for a walk.                            Ⓐ   Ⓑ   Ⓒ   Ⓓ   Ⓔ
```

In each of the following, use the correct form of the words in capitals to complete the sentence.

9  **GO   Mother has …… to the store.**                Ⓐ   Ⓑ   Ⓒ   Ⓓ   Ⓔ
   **A** went  **B** going  **C** goes  **D** gone  **E** goeth

0  **ABLE   We are confident you have the …… to do the**   Ⓐ   Ⓑ   Ⓒ   Ⓓ   Ⓔ
   **job.**
   **A** ableness  **B** ability  **C** ables  **D** enable  **E** disable

1  **ARRIVE   He is …… at noon today.**                Ⓐ   Ⓑ   Ⓒ   Ⓓ   Ⓔ
   **A** arriving  **B** arrives  **C** arrove  **D** arrival
   **E** arrived

2  **ATTRACT   The most …… girl won the contest.**     Ⓐ   Ⓑ   Ⓒ   Ⓓ   Ⓔ
   **A** attracts  **B** attractive  **C** attraction  **D** attracted
   **E** distract

3  **ADOPT   The baby was …… from birth.**             Ⓐ   Ⓑ   Ⓒ   Ⓓ   Ⓔ
   **A** adoption  **B** adopts  **C** adopted  **D** adopting
   **E** given

4  **CHOOSE   You have the …… of swimming or tennis.** Ⓐ   Ⓑ   Ⓒ   Ⓓ   Ⓔ
   **A** chose  **B** choose  **C** choice  **D** chosen  **E** chooses

5  **CRUEL   The older boy was punished for …… to the**  Ⓐ   Ⓑ   Ⓒ   Ⓓ   Ⓔ
   **younger one.**
   **A** cruelness  **B** cruelly  **C** cruelful  **D** cruelty
   **E** cruelled

6  **SUCCESS   Dane was …… in the examination.**       Ⓐ   Ⓑ   Ⓒ   Ⓓ   Ⓔ
   **A** successive  **B** successes  **C** succeed
   **D** successful  **E** sure

7  **BRING   He …… his pet rabbit to school.**         Ⓐ   Ⓑ   Ⓒ   Ⓓ   Ⓔ
   **A** brought  **B** bringeth  **C** bringing  **D** broughted
   **E** brung

78 **ACT**   I will await further ...... on the matter.
**A** active   **B** acts   **C** action   **D** acting   **E** acted

Ⓐ Ⓑ Ⓒ Ⓓ Ⓔ

79 **LIVE**   Old Mr Brown ...... on this street.
**A** living   **B** lives   **C** life   **D** alive   **E** lifes

Ⓐ Ⓑ Ⓒ Ⓓ Ⓔ

80 **LAUGH**   There was a shout of ...... from the room.
**A** laughter   **B** laughing   **C** laughs   **D** laughed
**E** jokes

Ⓐ Ⓑ Ⓒ Ⓓ Ⓔ

81 **FREE**   The man was ...... after he was found to be
**innocent.**
**A** freedom   **B** frees   **C** freed   **D** freeing   **E** fright

Ⓐ Ⓑ Ⓒ Ⓓ Ⓔ

In each of the following choose the correct word to fill the
blank.

82 **I do not agree ...... you on the matter.**
**A** to   **B** with   **C** for   **D** in   **E** at

Ⓐ Ⓑ Ⓒ Ⓓ Ⓔ

83 **They ran ...... the field during the game.**
**A** under   **B** through   **C** across   **D** over   **E** between

Ⓐ Ⓑ Ⓒ Ⓓ Ⓔ

84 **She went to the pond where the cows come ...... drink.**
**A** by   **B** for   **C** into   **D** to   **E** over

Ⓐ Ⓑ Ⓒ Ⓓ Ⓔ

85 **He had to apologise ...... his teacher.**
**A** before   **B** on   **C** to   **D** for   **E** with

Ⓐ Ⓑ Ⓒ Ⓓ Ⓔ

86 **His house is ...... the road.**
**A** at   **B** beside   **C** under   **D** into   **E** beneath

Ⓐ Ⓑ Ⓒ Ⓓ Ⓔ

87 **The river runs ...... the corn field.**
**A** around   **B** into   **C** on   **D** in   **E** through

Ⓐ Ⓑ Ⓒ Ⓓ Ⓔ

88 **He ran ...... the car and was injured.**
**A** by   **B** beside   **C** above   **D** into   **E** beyond

Ⓐ Ⓑ Ⓒ Ⓓ Ⓔ

89 **She is conscious ...... her shabby clothes.**
**A** with   **B** by   **C** off   **D** over   **E** of

Ⓐ Ⓑ Ⓒ Ⓓ Ⓔ

90 **She fell ...... the river and got soaking wet.**
**A** into   **B** through   **C** out   **D** on   **E** upon

Ⓐ Ⓑ Ⓒ Ⓓ Ⓔ

91 **He jumped ...... the wall and ran.**
**A** on   **B** in   **C** through   **D** into   **E** over

Ⓐ Ⓑ Ⓒ Ⓓ Ⓔ

# Nelson Caribbean

# Multiple Choice Tests for Common Entrance

## English

A B C D E

## Answer Key

(These four pages contain answers and may be removed from the main book at the teacher's discretion.)

Nelson Thornes

| | 1 | 2 | 3 | 4 | 5 | 6 | 7 | 8 | | 1 | 2 | 3 | 4 | 5 | 6 | 7 | 8 |
|---|---|---|---|---|---|---|---|---|---|---|---|---|---|---|---|---|---|
| 1 | C | A | C | C | E | A | E | D | 21 | B | D | B | D | A | E | D | C |
| 2 | A | C | C | A | A | D | D | D | 22 | A | E | E | C | A | A | A | A |
| 3 | D | B | B | C | B | C | B | B | 23 | B | C | A | B | D | A | E | C |
| 4 | E | B | A | B | A | C | E | D | 24 | A | B | E | C | E | E | B | C |
| 5 | A | B | B | B | A | B | D | D | 25 | D | C | D | C | D | C | C | C |
| 6 | A | D | B | D | C | A | A | E | 26 | A | B | E | A | C | A | B | B |
| 7 | D | C | A | B | B | B | A | C | 27 | B | E | A | B | A | C | A | C |
| 8 | A | E | A | D | C | A | C | C | 28 | B | A | E | B | C | D | C | C |
| 9 | C | B | C | B | D | E | D | C | 29 | A | D | C | C | B | B | B | D |
| 10 | B | D | A | E | C | C | C | C | 30 | C | B | A | D | E | E | B | C |
| 11 | C | A | B | C | B | B | A | D | 31 | D | A | D | C | B | D | D | B |
| 12 | D | C | B | A | A | C | D | B | 32 | A | D | B | A | D | A | A | C |
| 13 | D | D | B | D | D | E | B | D | 33 | C | A | C | B | D | C | C | A |
| 14 | B | D | A | B | B | E | C | A | 34 | A | D | C | C | C | E | D | C |
| 15 | A | E | B | E | E | C | D | D | 35 | C | A | B | B | C | B | A | D |
| 16 | D | A | E | A | C | E | E | C | 36 | B | E | A | D | D | A | D | E |
| 17 | A | B | E | C | D | E | C | B | 37 | C | C | B | E | B | B | A | C |
| 18 | B | D | C | D | E | B | E | C | 38 | A | A | C | A | B | A | B | B |
| 19 | C | E | B | B | D | C | A | A | 39 | B | B | B | D | E | B | B | B |
| 20 | C | A | E | A | E | B | D | B | 40 | C | D | B | A | A | B | A | B |

|    | 1 | 2 | 3 | 4 | 5 | 6 | 7 | 8 |    | 1 | 2 | 3 | 4 | 5 | 6 | 7 | 8 |
|----|---|---|---|---|---|---|---|---|----|---|---|---|---|---|---|---|---|
| 41 | A | B | B | C | D | D | A | C | 61 | D | D | C | A | A | D | B | A |
| 42 | C | A | B | B | B | A | E | C | 62 | A | C | C | D | E | C | B | D |
| 43 | B | D | A | A | D | C | A | C | 63 | B | A | C | E | C | A | C | B |
| 44 | B | E | C | B | A | C | C | E | 64 | C | B | C | D | A | A | E | A |
| 45 | B | A | C | D | E | C | C | E | 65 | A | C | C | B | D | C | B | A |
| 46 | D | B | B | B | B | D | C | B | 66 | D | C | A | A | A | B | D | C |
| 47 | A | D | A | A | E | C | D | A | 67 | C | B | E | B | B | B | E | B |
| 48 | D | D | A | D | A | B | A | B | 68 | B | E | A | C | C | C | C | A |
| 49 | B | A | D | E | D | C | D | C | 69 | E | C | A | B | E | C | D | D |
| 50 | D | D | C | D | E | D | B | C | 70 | D | B | B | A | A | B | B | C |
| 51 | A | B | D | C | C | D | C | B | 71 | A | E | A | D | B | C | A | A |
| 52 | C | C | B | B | E | C | E | C | 72 | D | B | A | A | C | C | B | B |
| 53 | E | B | E | C | A | D | A | A | 73 | C | E | B | B | C | E | C | C |
| 54 | B | E | A | D | C | D | C | C | 74 | D | D | D | A | D | B | C | C |
| 55 | D | C | D | A | B | C | A | D | 75 | A | B | E | D | B | C | D | A |
| 56 | A | A | C | C | B | D | A | A | 76 | B | A | C | C | A | D | D | B |
| 57 | B | E | B | D | A | B | D | A | 77 | D | D | A | A | D | E | A | E |
| 58 | B | D | A | A | B | B | E | E | 78 | A | E | A | B | B | C | C | C |
| 59 | D | B | C | D | B | A | D | B | 79 | B | B | C | C | E | B | A |   |
| 60 | B | A | D | B | B | C | C | A | 80 | A | D | C | B | A | B | A | A |

|     | 1 | 2 | 3 | 4 | 5 | 6 | 7 | 8 |     | 1 | 2 | 3 | 4 | 5 | 6 | 7 | 8 |
|-----|---|---|---|---|---|---|---|---|-----|---|---|---|---|---|---|---|---|
| 81  | C | B | B | D | C | E | C | C | 91  | C | A | E | C | B | A | E | B |
| 82  | B | A | A | C | D | A | B | B | 92  | A | D | E | B | B | A | A | D |
| 83  | A | C | B | C | B | B | C | A | 93  | C | B | B | C | A | B | D | E |
| 84  | C | D | D | D | C | C | D | B | 94  | A | D | E | C | B | C | B | C |
| 85  | C | E | A | C | D | D | C | C | 95  | B | C | C | C | D | A | C | E |
| 86  | A | A | A | E | A | B | B | A | 96  | A | E | A | A | A | E | D | B |
| 87  | B | E | D | E | C | C | E | C | 97  | B | B | A | A | E | A | E | A |
| 88  | B | A | B | B | D | B | D | B | 98  | A | C | B | B | B | D | C | B |
| 89  | C | C | A | D | B | C | E | C | 99  | B | A | C | A | D | E | A | A |
| 90  | D | D | A | A | C | C | A | A | 100 | C | C | B | C | C | C | C | B |

In each of the following choose the best expression.

2  A  The market is crowded on Saturdays. ✓
   B  Big crowds reach the markets on Saturdays. ✗
   C  Many people crowd up the markets on Saturdays. ✓
   D  People full up the market on Saturdays. ✗
   E  On Saturdays the market are full of people. ✓

   (A)  (B)  (C)  (D)  (E)

3  A  At the bus stop the people just crowd up.
   B  People must learn to line up at the bus stop.
   C  People really, awful at the bus stop.
   D  People do not make orderly lines at the bus stop.
   E  People just bundle up at the bus stop.

   (A)  (B)  (C)  (D)  (E)

4  A  I can do anything for you lady?
   B  May I help you, madam?
   C  What you want ma'am?
   D  You want something lady?
   E  Is what you want ma'am?

   (A)  (B)  (C)  (D)  (E)

5  A  People just walk all over the road.
   B  People don't even know how to walk on road.
   C  People are careless when walking on the road.
   D  People everywhere over the road.
   E  People believe car not to drive on the road.

   (A)  (B)  (C)  (D)  (E)

6  A  The mini buses really pack up bad.
   B  The mini buses pack up bad.
   C  The mini buses really awful.
   D  The mini buses are badly overcrowded.
   E  People just squeeze up in the mini buses.

   (A)  (B)  (C)  (D)  (E)

7  A  The drivers drive too bad on the roads.
   B  Drivers just gallop on the roads.
   C  The drivers think the road is for them alone.
   D  Some drivers don't know how to drive on the roads.
   E  There is too much reckless driving on the roads.

   (A)  (B)  (C)  (D)  (E)

8  A  The goods in the shop but no money.
   B  Plenty goods in the shops but things bad.
   C  The goods are available but money is in short supply.
   D  Plenty things on the shelves but times hard.
   E  Money hard to get nowadays to buy what you want.

   (A)  (B)  (C)  (D)  (E)

**99**   **A**   The heavy rains flooded the roads.
       **B**   The heavy rains filled up the roads with water.
       **C**   The roads were all flooded up by the heavy rains.
       **D**   The heavy rains make the roads flood.
       **E**   The heavy rains cover all the roads.

                                                     (A)   (B)   (C)   (D)   (E)

**100**   **A**   The children was playing happily when the bell rang.
       **B**   The bell ring as the children playing happily.
       **C**   The children were playing happily when the bell rang.
       **D**   The bell had to ring as the children were happily
           playing.
       **E**   The children happily playing when the bell go and
           ring.

                                                       (A)   (B)   (C)   (D)   (E)

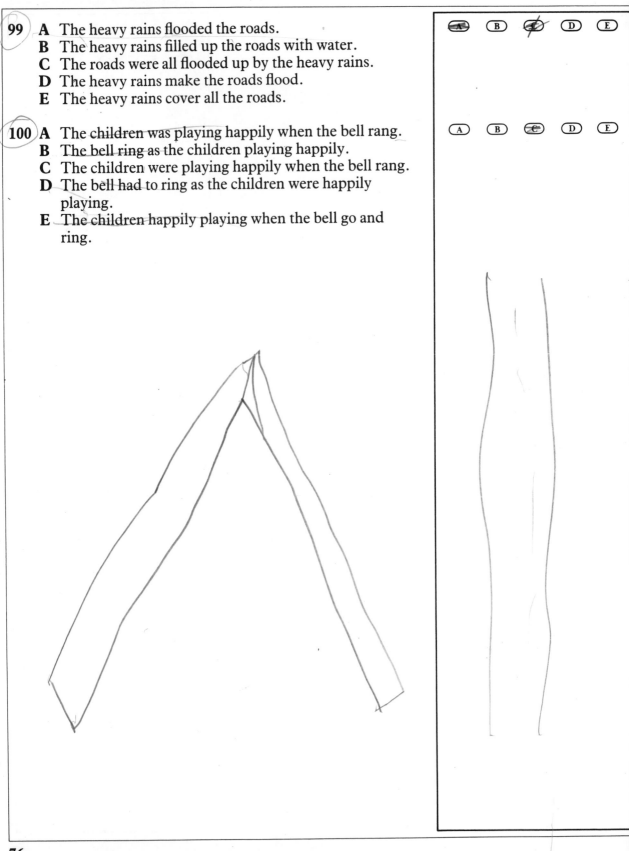

# PAPER EIGHT

Read the following passage carefully then choose the correct
answer.

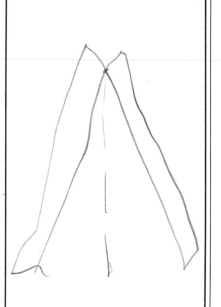

It was an unusually windy afternoon when the ominous clouds
were like mountains watching overhead. The retailers were
about to close their shutters after a very profitable day of
business. The busy hum of the streets was gradually lulling as
families had already collected the necessities they hoped would
last them during the pending disaster. A few villagers could be
seen and heard hammering to make their homes more secure.
Ears were glued to the radio sets as the radio stations busily
gave half-hourly bulletins to keep the listeners vigilant and up
to date.

1.  **Ominous means the same as**
    **A** brightly coloured   **B** low   **C** feathery
    **D** threatening   **E** gigantic
    ⓐ ⓑ ⓒ ⓓ ⓔ

2   **The retailers can be considered as**
    **A** consumers   **B** buyers   **C** wholesalers
    **D** merchants   **E** clerks
    ⓐ ⓑ ⓒ ⓓ ⓔ

3   **Lulling means the same as**
    **A** beginning   **B** subsiding   **C** rising   **D** selling
    **E** buzzing
    ⓐ ⓑ ⓒ ⓓ ⓔ

4   **Necessities refer to**
    **A** foodstuffs   **B** tools   **C** bits of information   **D** basic
    needs   **E** unnecessary needs
    ⓐ ⓑ ⓒ ⓓ ⓔ

5   **Pending means the same as**
    **A** passing   **B** ending   **C** continuing   **D** oncoming
    **E** resisting
    ⓐ ⓑ ⓒ ⓓ ⓔ

6   **Ears were glued to the radio because**
    **A** the villagers like to listen to the news
    **B** people could not view the news
    **C** there was nothing else to listen to
    **D** there was nothing left to be done
    **E** information was vital
    ⓐ ⓑ ⓒ ⓓ ⓔ

**7** **Half-hourly means**
   **A** once in every two hours
   **B** twice in every hour and a half
   **C** twice in every hour
   **D** twice in every thirty minutes   **E** biannually

Ⓐ  Ⓑ  Ⓒ  Ⓓ  Ⓔ

**8** **The disaster referred to in the passage is an approaching**
   **A** earthquake   **B** volcano   **C** hurricane
   **D** cloud seeding   **E** traffic accident

Ⓐ  Ⓑ  Ⓒ  Ⓓ  Ⓔ

In each of the following, choose the letter of the word that means the same or nearly the same as the word underlined.

**9** **The heavy clouds warned that rain was imminent.**
   **A** falling   **B** dewing   **C** about to fall   **D** flooding
   **E** damaging

Ⓐ  Ⓑ  Ⓒ  Ⓓ  Ⓔ

**10** **Mother takes pleasure in rearing miniature roses.**
   **A** hybrid   **B** variegated   **C** small   **D** pink   **E** large

Ⓐ  Ⓑ  Ⓒ  Ⓓ  Ⓔ

**11** **A lively trade in footwear is carried on in the markets.**
   **A** happy   **B** profitable   **C** illegal   **D** brisk   **E** slow

Ⓐ  Ⓑ  Ⓒ  Ⓓ  Ⓔ

**12** **The goods are attractively displayed on the sidewalks.**
   **A** distributed   **B** shown   **C** seen   **D** wrapped
   **E** hung

Ⓐ  Ⓑ  Ⓒ  Ⓓ  Ⓔ

**13** **I will represent the group, provided you supply the necessary information.**
   **A** while   **B** since   **C** because   **D** if   **E** though

Ⓐ  Ⓑ  Ⓒ  Ⓓ  Ⓔ

**14** **He worked hard in order to acquire a skill in computer programming.**
   **A** get   **B** find   **C** have   **D** buy   **E** teach

Ⓐ  Ⓑ  Ⓒ  Ⓓ  Ⓔ

**15** **A peculiar old man inched his way through the crowd.**
   **A** dwarf   **B** ugly   **C** old   **D** strange   **E** lonely

Ⓐ  Ⓑ  Ⓒ  Ⓓ  Ⓔ

**16** **It appeared as if labour disputes would never end.**
   **A** meant   **B** rose   **C** seemed   **D** occurred   **E** showed

Ⓐ  Ⓑ  Ⓒ  Ⓓ  Ⓔ

In each of the following, choose the correct spelling for the underlined word.

17  His **curiousity** was aroused.
    **A** curiousety  **B** curiosity  **C** couriosity
    **D** cueriosity  **E** kuriosity

    Ⓐ  Ⓑ  Ⓒ  Ⓓ  Ⓔ

18  I am greatly **indetted** to you.
    **A** indeted  **B** indeated  **C** indebted  **D** indatted
    **E** indeitted

    Ⓐ  Ⓑ  Ⓒ  Ⓓ  Ⓔ

19  The camper did not want to **loose** his way.
    **A** lose  **B** loss  **C** louse  **D** looce  **E** lews

    Ⓐ  Ⓑ  Ⓒ  Ⓓ  Ⓔ

20  The florist likes to **raer** his own flowers.
    **A** rarre  **B** rear  **C** raere  **D** rare  **E** rair

    Ⓐ  Ⓑ  Ⓒ  Ⓓ  Ⓔ

21  The **choffeur** was fined for overspeeding.
    **A** cihoffer  **B** choeffeur  **C** chauffeur  **D** chouffeur
    **E** choeffer

    Ⓐ  Ⓑ  Ⓒ  Ⓓ  Ⓔ

22  While travelling in the country areas, I enjoy the beautiful **seenery**.
    **A** scenery  **B** sceinry  **C** scienery  **D** senery
    **E** scenry

    Ⓐ  Ⓑ  Ⓒ  Ⓓ  Ⓔ

23  Mathematics is my favourite **subjek**.
    **A** subjict  **B** subjick  **C** subject  **D** subjekt
    **E** subjeck

    Ⓐ  Ⓑ  Ⓒ  Ⓓ  Ⓔ

24  The **vehycles** were seized by the examiner.
    **A** vecles  **B** vehecles  **C** vehicles  **D** veecles
    **E** veihicles

    Ⓐ  Ⓑ  Ⓒ  Ⓓ  Ⓔ

25  I do not **beleeve** the story.
    **A** beleefe  **B** beleave  **C** believe  **D** beleive
    **E** believ

    Ⓐ  Ⓑ  Ⓒ  Ⓓ  Ⓔ

Choose the correct letter for opposites of the words in capitals.

26  **ALLOW**
    **A** permit  **B** prevent  **C** encourage  **D** help
    **E** assist

    Ⓐ  Ⓑ  Ⓒ  Ⓓ  Ⓔ

27  **WEALTH**
    **A** riches  **B** poor  **C** poverty  **D** wisdom  **E** health

    Ⓐ  Ⓑ  Ⓒ  Ⓓ  Ⓔ

**28 SOME**
  **A** all   **B** few   **C** none   **D** many   **E** more

| Ⓐ | Ⓑ | Ⓒ | Ⓓ | Ⓔ |
|---|---|---|---|---|

**29 ENCOURAGE**
  **A** help   **B** disencourage   **C** prevent   **D** discourage
  **E** enhance

| Ⓐ | Ⓑ | Ⓒ | Ⓓ | Ⓔ |
|---|---|---|---|---|

**30 SWEET**
  **A** salty   **B** sugar   **C** sour   **D** candy   **E** vinegar

| Ⓐ | Ⓑ | Ⓒ | Ⓓ | Ⓔ |
|---|---|---|---|---|

**31 GIVE**
  **A** accept   **B** take   **C** lend   **D** buy   **E** have

| Ⓐ | Ⓑ | Ⓒ | Ⓓ | Ⓔ |
|---|---|---|---|---|

**32 DAMP**
  **A** cold   **B** wet   **C** dry   **D** humid   **E** dirty

| Ⓐ | Ⓑ | Ⓒ | Ⓓ | Ⓔ |
|---|---|---|---|---|

**33 NARROW**
  **A** wide   **B** large   **C** small   **D** big   **E** long

| Ⓐ | Ⓑ | Ⓒ | Ⓓ | Ⓔ |
|---|---|---|---|---|

**34 LAZY**
  **A** idle   **B** thrifty   **C** industrious   **D** swift   **E** slow

| Ⓐ | Ⓑ | Ⓒ | Ⓓ | Ⓔ |
|---|---|---|---|---|

**35 RAPID**
  **A** strange   **B** swift   **C** quick   **D** slow   **E** hard

| Ⓐ | Ⓑ | Ⓒ | Ⓓ | Ⓔ |
|---|---|---|---|---|

**36 PARDON**
  **A** forgive   **B** plead   **C** beg   **D** release   **E** blame

| Ⓐ | Ⓑ | Ⓒ | Ⓓ | Ⓔ |
|---|---|---|---|---|

In each of the following one of the words is used incorrectly,
find which one.

  **A  B      C      D       E**
**37**  Mary is the biggest of the two girls.

| Ⓐ | Ⓑ | Ⓒ | Ⓓ | Ⓔ |
|---|---|---|---|---|

  **A       B  C       D               E**
**38**  The man run when he realised that he had been
  discovered.

| Ⓐ | Ⓑ | Ⓒ | Ⓓ | Ⓔ |
|---|---|---|---|---|

  **A  B      C      D   E**
**39**  She past the package to me as I sat down.

| Ⓐ | Ⓑ | Ⓒ | Ⓓ | Ⓔ |
|---|---|---|---|---|

  **A      B    C D E**
**40**  Nobody know why he was late.

| Ⓐ | Ⓑ | Ⓒ | Ⓓ | Ⓔ |
|---|---|---|---|---|

|   | A | B | C | D | E |
|---|---|---|---|---|---|

**1** Each of the bags were filled with ripe oranges

    A    B     C  D    E

Ⓐ   Ⓑ   Ⓒ   Ⓓ   Ⓔ

**2** The girl, not her friends, were late for school.

Ⓐ   Ⓑ   Ⓒ   Ⓓ   Ⓔ

**3** Between you and I it was Jane who broke the jar.

Ⓐ   Ⓑ   Ⓒ   Ⓓ   Ⓔ

**4** Tom is much smaller than me.

Ⓐ   Ⓑ   Ⓒ   Ⓓ   Ⓔ

**5** The wounded man fell to the ground with a grown.

Ⓐ   Ⓑ   Ⓒ   Ⓓ   Ⓔ

**6** We must higher a car to take us home.

Ⓐ   Ⓑ   Ⓒ   Ⓓ   Ⓔ

In each of the following choose the word which correctly completes each sentence.

Ⓐ   Ⓑ   Ⓒ   Ⓓ   Ⓔ

**7** **The car was ......, it was unable to move.**
**A** stationary   **B** station   **C** fixing   **D** overhauled
**E** stationery

Ⓐ   Ⓑ   Ⓒ   Ⓓ   Ⓔ

**8** **The man was ...... of the theft of the diamond ring.**
**A** happy   **B** guilty   **C** found   **D** fond   **E** pretending

Ⓐ   Ⓑ   Ⓒ   Ⓓ   Ⓔ

**9** **The policeman had to ...... the princess as she walked down the street.**
**A** talk   **B** carry   **C** guard   **D** gaol   **E** bring

Ⓐ   Ⓑ   Ⓒ   Ⓓ   Ⓔ

**50** **There are many ...... people walking around on the streets.**
**A** instant   **B** instinct   **C** insane   **D** immediate
**E** infant

Ⓐ   Ⓑ   Ⓒ   Ⓓ   Ⓔ

**51** **The solution to that problem is quite ......**
**A** single   **B** simple   **C** sing   **D** sweet   **E** sample

Ⓐ   Ⓑ   Ⓒ   Ⓓ   Ⓔ

**52** **The job is ...... but I like it.**
**A** diverse   **B** defeat   **C** difficult   **D** diffuse   **E** dear

Ⓐ   Ⓑ   Ⓒ   Ⓓ   Ⓔ

**53** **The doctor arrived late so his ...... waited.**
**A** patients   **B** patent   **C** patience   **D** pair
**E** poverty

Ⓐ   Ⓑ   Ⓒ   Ⓓ   Ⓔ

**54** The grocer will ...... the goods I ordered.　　Ⓐ Ⓑ Ⓒ Ⓓ Ⓔ
　　**A** divide　**B** decide　**C** deliver　**D** different
　　**E** define

**55** We are friends but we do not ...... the same school.　　Ⓐ Ⓑ Ⓒ Ⓓ Ⓔ
　　**A** advance　**B** advice　**C** adhere　**D** attend　**E** alone

Read the following passage carefully then choose the letter that correctly answers each question.

The most glorious example of the variety and colour of Trinidadian culture is the annual national festival of carnival. This tradition originated with the French settlers in the island. On the two days preceding Ash Wednesday, carnival in Trinidad has come to be one of the most splendid and enjoyable events in the world. The colourful costumes and themes paraded on these days are often a clear indication of the many origins and wide interests of the people. During carnival, Trinidadians of all races come together as one as they dance and sing to the calypso music which reverberates throughout the land.

**56** The most glorious example of Trinidadian culture is　　Ⓐ Ⓑ Ⓒ Ⓓ Ⓔ
　　best displayed in
　　**A** the national festival of carnival
　　**B** the variety and colour　**C** calypso music
　　**D** tradition　**E** French settlers

**57** Culture is　　Ⓐ Ⓑ Ⓒ Ⓓ Ⓔ
　　**A** a life style　**B** food　**C** people　**D** interest
　　**E** music

**58** Trinidadians descend from　　Ⓐ Ⓑ Ⓒ Ⓓ Ⓔ
　　**A** Africans only　**B** Indians only　**C** Europeans only
　　**D** Asians　**E** many races

**59** Preceding means　　Ⓐ Ⓑ Ⓒ Ⓓ Ⓔ
　　**A** following　**B** before　**C** like　**D** around　**E** called

**60** One of the major attractions at carnival is　　Ⓐ Ⓑ Ⓒ Ⓓ Ⓔ
　　**A** the colourful costumes
　　**B** the interest of the people　**C** the singing
　　**D** the food　**E** the people watching

**61** 'Reverberates' means the same as
A resounds   B music   C noisy   D loud   E walks

A B C D E

**62** Carnival was first started by
A the Indians   B the Negroes   C the Africans
D the French settlers   E the races

A B C D E

**63** 'Originated' means the same as
A ended   B began   C followed   D made
E endured

A B C D E

**64** Carnival serves to
A unite all races in celebration
B cause strife among races   C make people unhappy
D cause confusion   E make Trinidadians lazy

A B C D E

In each of the following sentences choose the form of the word
in capitals that best completes each sentence.

**65** MAKE   She …… all my dresses.
A makes   B sews   C making   D machined   E gave

A B C D E

**66** THROW   The ball was …… through the window.
A throwing   B flung   C thrown   D threw
E throws

A B C D E

**67** MOUNTAIN   This is a …… country.
A mountaineer   B mountainous   C mounting
D mountained   E mount

A B C D E

**68** SELECT   She …… the best apples from the basket.
A selected   B selecting   C chose   D selection
E buy

A B C D E

**69** VISIT   They are frequent …… to our house.
A visits   B visiting   C visited   D visitors
E visitation

A B C D E

**70** INFORM   My …… is, that he will arrive tomorrow.
A informant   B informed   C information
D informing   E informal

A B C D E

**71** ASSIST   The passerby quickly came to my …… when
I was attacked.
A assistance   B assisted   C assistant   D help
E assisting

A B C D E

83

72 **CHOOSE** Tom was ...... to represent his school at the ceremony.
**A** chose  **B** chosen  **C** selected  **D** choice
**E** choosing

Ⓐ Ⓑ Ⓒ Ⓓ Ⓔ

73 **CHILD** His ...... behaviour got him into trouble with his superiors.
**A** childhood  **B** children  **C** childish  **D** fun
**E** childless

Ⓐ Ⓑ Ⓒ Ⓓ Ⓔ

74 **DO** Why ...... you remove the book from the table?
**A** done  **B** does  **C** did  **D** doing  **E** doth

Ⓐ Ⓑ Ⓒ Ⓓ Ⓔ

In each of the following, choose the sentence correctly punctuated.

75 **A** 'Let's get out of here!' exclaimed the frightened boy.
**B** 'Lets get out of here!' exclaimed the frightened boy.
**C** 'Let's get out of here exclaimed the frightened boy'
**D** 'Lets get out of here.' exclaimed the frightened boy.
**E** 'Let's get out of here,' exclaimed the frightened boy.

Ⓐ Ⓑ Ⓒ Ⓓ Ⓔ

76 **A** 'Are you coming to the party tomorrow.'
**B** 'Are you coming to the party tomorrow?'
**C** Are you coming to the party tomorrow?
**D** Are you coming to the party tomorrow.
**E** Are you coming to the party tomorrow

Ⓐ Ⓑ Ⓒ Ⓓ Ⓔ

77 **A** Dinner is ready, called mother, please come to the table.
**B** 'Dinner is ready called mother please come to the table.'
**C** 'Dinner is ready', called mother please come to the table.
**D** 'Dinner is ready' called mother 'please come to the table.'
**E** 'Dinner is ready,' called mother, 'please come to the table.'

Ⓐ Ⓑ Ⓒ Ⓓ Ⓔ

78 **A** Mr Jones my father's friend came to visit us.
**B** Mr Jones, my fathers friend, came to visit us.
**C** Mr Jones, my father's friend, came to visit us.
**D** Mr Jones my fathers friend, came to visit us!
**E** Mr Jones, my fathers' friend, came to visit us.

Ⓐ Ⓑ Ⓒ Ⓓ Ⓔ

79 **A** There was a loud rumble; then the world seemed to explode around us.
   **B** There was a loud rumble, then the world seemed to explode around us.
   **C** There was a loud rumble, then the world seemed, to explode around us.
   **D** There was a loud rumble then the world seemed to explode around us.
   **E** 'There was a loud rumble then the world seemed to explode around us.'

   Ⓐ Ⓑ Ⓒ Ⓓ Ⓔ

80 **A** On the table, were books, pens, pencils, erasers and boxes of crayons.
   **B** On the table were books pens pencils erasers and boxes of crayons.
   **C** On the table were books, pens, pencils, erasers, and boxes of crayons
   **D** On the table were books pens, pencils erasers, and boxes of crayons.
   **E** On the table were, books, pens, pencils erasers, and boxes of crayons

   Ⓐ Ⓑ Ⓒ Ⓓ Ⓔ

In each of the following choose the word that correctly completes each phrase.

81 **walked ...... the corner with a friend**
   **A** in   **B** into   **C** around   **D** over   **E** under

   Ⓐ Ⓑ Ⓒ Ⓓ Ⓔ

82 **disappeared ...... the bushes**
   **A** around   **B** into   **C** by   **D** from   **E** up

   Ⓐ Ⓑ Ⓒ Ⓓ Ⓔ

83 **walked ...... the two cars**
   **A** between   **B** over   **C** under   **D** into   **E** up

   Ⓐ Ⓑ Ⓒ Ⓓ Ⓔ

84 **dived ...... water**
   **A** about   **B** into   **C** over   **D** across   **E** above

   Ⓐ Ⓑ Ⓒ Ⓓ Ⓔ

85 **sat ...... the chair**
   **A** into   **B** upon   **C** on   **D** under   **E** at

   Ⓐ Ⓑ Ⓒ Ⓓ Ⓔ

86 **looked ...... to the sky**
   **A** up   **B** over   **C** between   **D** beyond   **E** during

   Ⓐ Ⓑ Ⓒ Ⓓ Ⓔ

87 **broke his arm ...... the match**
   **A** by   **B** because   **C** during   **D** from   **E** off

   Ⓐ Ⓑ Ⓒ Ⓓ Ⓔ

**88** ashamed ...... your poor behaviour
A by   B of   C over   D into   E with

A⃝  B⃝  C⃝  D⃝  E⃝

Choose the word that means the same or nearly the same as the words in capitals.

**89 FINISH**
A stop   B start   C end   D go   E begin

A⃝  B⃝  C⃝  D⃝  E⃝

**90 STAMINA**
A strength   B speed   C weakness   D slow   E race

A⃝  B⃝  C⃝  D⃝  E⃝

**91 CAUTION**
A rashness   B care   C careless   D slowly   E skill

A⃝  B⃝  C⃝  D⃝  E⃝

**92 FUNCTIONS**
A machine   B fair   C fail   D works   E neglect

A⃝  B⃝  C⃝  D⃝  E⃝

**93 APPAREL**
A pale   B notice   C apple   D cotton   E clothes

A⃝  B⃝  C⃝  D⃝  E⃝

**94 LOFTY**
A clear   B crowd   C high   D low   E humble

A⃝  B⃝  C⃝  D⃝  E⃝

**95 BLUNDER**
A happiness   B burn   C accuracy   D dull
E mistake

A⃝  B⃝  C⃝  D⃝  E⃝

**96 CONCISE**
A clear   B brief   C clean   D add   E wise

A⃝  B⃝  C⃝  D⃝  E⃝

**97 SUMMIT**
A top   B sky   C call   D base   E cloudy

A⃝  B⃝  C⃝  D⃝  E⃝

**98 PLACID**
A beauty   B mild   C careful   D royal   E tantrum

A⃝  B⃝  C⃝  D⃝  E⃝

**99 RARE**
A seldom found   B raw   C lift   D common
E many

A⃝  B⃝  C⃝  D⃝  E⃝

**100 FRANK**
A fresh   B candid   C foster   D secretive   E story

A⃝  B⃝  C⃝  D⃝  E⃝